Prague Spring

Prague Spring

Z. A. B. Zeman

 Hill and Wang   *New York*

For Anthea

Contents

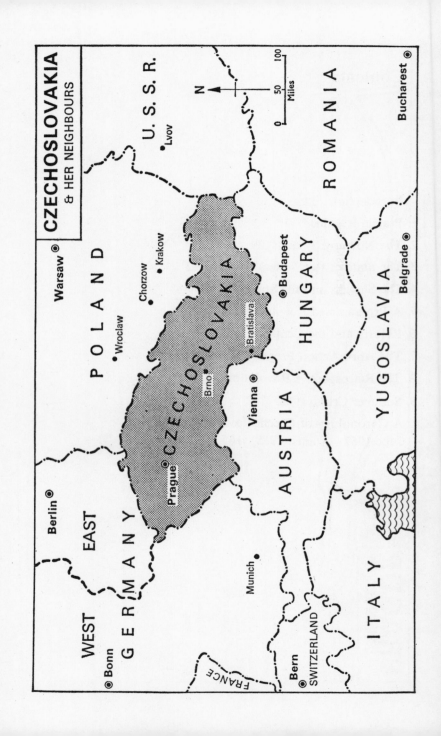

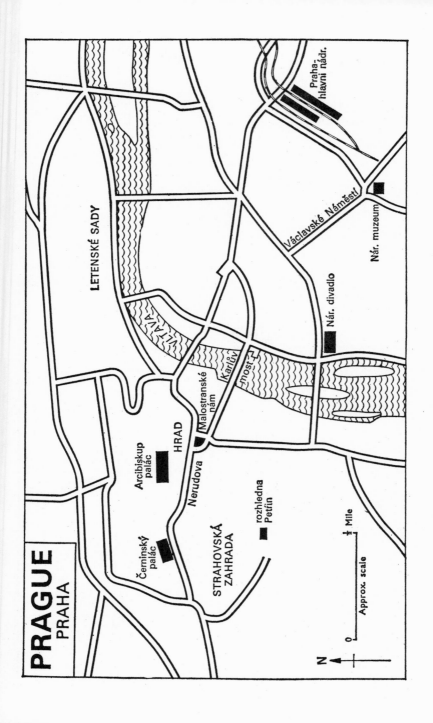

Introduction

The book before you analyses the causes and the course of the
Czechoslovak communist reform movement. It is not called
'the rape of Czechoslovakia' or 'the end of a dream', nor does
it purvey that kind of a message. I started writing it when I
returned from Prague in April 1968 and finished it in July.
After the August invasion of Czechoslovakia, I added a few
pages to the last chapter. All the other chapters remain un-
changed.

The Czechs had found themselves involved in a similar
brawl once before. In the fifteenth century Jan Hus and his
followers attacked the late medieval church, and the whole
nation became drawn into a clash with a powerful and corrupt
institution. They anticipated the general European reforma-
tion by a century.

The present quarrel of the Czechs and the Slovaks is basically with the way states are run. They have assumed that 'we
are not born in order to be governed easily'. Other communists before them, men like President Tito and Chairman Mao,
had asserted the right of their countries to independence from
Moscow. But 'polycentrism' is not really the point the Czechs
are making. They have glanced back at the cruelty the communists had committed against each other, and shuddered.
They have put forward incisive views on the relationship
between tight bureaucratic control and the development of
material and spiritual values. They have shown that absolute
power not only corrupts but that it never is accompanied by
absolute responsibility. They started dismantling the heavy
bureaucratic machinery of the party and the state.

The Hungarian revolution of 1956 was a passionate, emotional occasion and received a similar kind of response. The Czechoslovak reform movement is more of an intellectual exercise. Even under extreme pressure the Czechs and the Slovaks kept their emotions in the background as much as they could. They negotiated, argued, ridiculed. They have not given up hope yet.

The Russians and their allies have it in their power to delay, and perhaps destroy, the Czechoslovak reform movement. If they set out on that course they will find it impossible to achieve even the 'silent consensus' that John Locke believed necessary for government. They will meet with the sullen silence of an indifferent, conquered people. The Czechs and the Slovaks will become consumers of wheat and inefficient producers of steel, occasionally communicating with each other in a quaint dialect of the western Slavs.

1. Prague Regained

Czechoslovakia was the last country to disappear, in 1948, into Stalin's east European empire. After the dictator's death in 1953 Stalinism survived there longer than anywhere else. There was rioting in East Germany in the same year. In 1956 Khruschchev made his historic speech on the abuses of Stalin's regime to the twentieth party congress in Moscow. There was a revolt in Poland and a revolution in Hungary. Russian tanks blasted the revolutionaries in Budapest; in Warsaw, Gomulka emerged as the new party leader. All this time the government in Prague remained solid, unshaken. The biggest statue of Stalin anywhere in the world looked down on the capital; the Czechs acquired a reputation for a perverse, inhuman kind of stability. In the past three or four years the severe face their government presented to the outside world began to lose some of its grimness. A few novels appeared, bearing the mark of authenticity; a few films reached western audiences that spoke in direct, unpolitical language; coach-loads of Czechs came to watch ice-hockey matches in Vienna. And all the while, there was something very wrong with the Czechoslovak economy.

In January 1968 the whole façade began to collapse. Antonín Novotný, the first secretary of the party of more than fourteen years' standing, was replaced by Alexander Dubček, an unknown Slovak. Novotný remained the President of the Republic, but not for long. A high-ranking general escaped to America and the official explanation (big speculative deals in clover seed) brightened up the mood of the people for a while. The political scene looked as if whoever was manipulating the puppets had suddenly let go of all the strings. Resignations, suicides, public inquiries followed each other in rapid succession. Another meeting of the central committee of the Communist Party was arranged for the beginning of April. Soviet troops in Hungary and East Germany were on the move again, reported to be observing strict radio silence, their tanks getting tangled up with the tourist traffic between Vienna and Budapest.

Was there a revolution taking place in Prague? The news reaching western capitals in the first months of the year indicated that such might be the case. By the end of March, the changes in Czechoslovakia appeared more far-reaching than anything that had happened in the communist countries of eastern Europe since the end of the war. The Czechs were being highly articulate about the events in their country, they seemed to know what they wanted, and there had been no violence. I interrupted the work I was then doing in Vienna, and went to find out for myself. I had not visited Prague, my native town, for twenty years.

The Franz Josef Bahnhof, a station in Vienna built to serve traffic with the western provinces of the Habsburg Empire, now looks small and neglected. Early in the morning, shabby trains bring in commuters from the outer suburbs. The Vindobona Express provided a sharp contrast. There it was, at the far platform, almost empty, streamlined and powerful, its air-conditioning plant gently humming. I got on it shortly after eight o'clock on 2 April 1968. It left Vienna on time at 8.10 a.m. and crossed the Czech frontier two hours later. It made its way through familiar countryside. The dark ponds of south Bohemia, built by monks to breed carp, food for the feasts and fasts; then Tábor, the fortress town of the religious wars in the fifteenth century. In the rolling, fertile country of central Bohemia the train slowed down. There were hundreds of troops repairing the track; the grass on the banks along the railway line had been burnt down and in places it was smoking, or still on fire. Most of the engines we saw on the way were powered by steam. As we approached Prague we entered the miniature country: small hills with little white churches at the top; tiny ponds and tight, wooded valleys; clusters of log cabins on the river Sázava, where town people spend their summer week-ends. And finally, early in the afternoon, the Prague suburbs, the long tunnel – the beginning of many childhood holidays – and the platforms of the central station under the customary big-span glass and iron arches.

There were no porters about and only one taxi outside the station; an old, battered Russian Volga. The taxi driver said he would take me to the central accommodation office instead of driving me from one hotel to another, getting, as he put it, more and more depressed, and ending up somewhere in the outer suburbs. He asked me whether I was an Arctic explorer. It seemed that he had recently driven one, who had spent several years somewhere near the North Pole, and 'spoke Czech in the same stiff way as you do'.

I got the last room that was to be had in Prague, with three beds in it, at a hotel near the station. Between the wars, it was used by travelling salesmen down on their luck. It never had a chance to become really popular. Sleeping there was like having a bed in the middle of the platform, with engines shunting alongside it, slowly and thoughtfully, the whole night. The following day I moved to a large, comfortable hotel in a north-western suburb. Incredibly ugly, the building had been originally intended for the entertainment of military visitors from the Warsaw Pact countries. The former Minister of Defence responsible for it now lives nearby, with the slab-like evidence of his departed power daily before his eyes.

My first impression of Prague was terrible. The once pleasant park outside the railway station was dug up, and little boys played football on a small plot of hard, yellow soil. An incongruous ferro-concrete building was going up near the National Museum. The Václavské náměstí, the square gently sloping towards the centre of the town, was full of people in the middle of a working afternoon. The trees that used to line the square had disappeared; large sections of the pavements on its two sides were boarded off, and pedestrians had to use the arcades that link the houses on the square with the neighbouring streets. The people were preoccupied and grim, and I caught occasional glimpses of armed troops, walking slowly in pairs. The whole scene was surrounded by a film of fine dust.

I remembered a sentence I had read a few days before, in an article by Hugh Trevor-Roper on Philby in *Encounter* (March 1968), describing how twenty years of communist rule had turned the capital of Czechoslovakia, a kind of Switzerland before the war, into a central European slum. Long, silent queues were waiting for the evening newspaper. I bought a copy and went back to the hotel to read it.

In the evening, I walked up to the castle; it was dark when I got there. Two motionless guards, submachine guns across their chests, stood at the gate. The first courtyard was dimly lit, and deserted; brighter lights and some activity – the black fish-shaped Tatra cars arriving and leaving in quick succession – was going on under the archway of the King Matthias' gate. The plenum of the central committee of the Communist Party was meeting in the Spanish Hall, above the gate: the broad marble staircase leading up to it was lined with banks of spring flowers and covered with the inevitable red carpet. I knew well the view of the staircase and of the glass door at the end of the landing, but I was aware that somehow it was out of alignment, that there was something subtly wrong with it.

That feeling, produced by the superimposition of the image retained by the eye of memory on the present, very similar, but not quite the same picture, returned again and again during the first days of my stay in Prague. It had a disturbing quality about it which could be removed, as I soon found out, by exercising hard one's memory. Indeed I had seen that staircase, red-carpeted and lined with flowers, as a small boy, more than thirty years ago. But it was then full of people. In the summer of 1937, in the hall beyond the tall glass door, Thomas Masaryk, the founder and the first President of the Czechoslovak Republic, was lying in state. Tonight, shortly before eight o'clock in the evening, the staircase was empty. From time to time a member of the central committee of the party slowly walked down it, got into a black Tatra car, and was driven away.

The second courtyard was quiet, its renaissance fountain turned off and the chapel of the Holy Cross locked up for the night; official cars were parked in the third courtyard, dominated by the cathedral. Some of the drivers were talking softly, and others dozed behind the wheels. I turned back and started walking down the hill towards Malá Strana. Half-way down the winding, steep street a solitary student was making a mocking speech ('I too admit to having made dreadful mistakes in the past . . .') from a balcony above the door to a wine cellar.

Slowly the town was coming back into focus; although it took several days to dispel the unfavourable impression of the first few hours of my stay in Prague. It has in fact changed much less than London in the past twenty years. Apart from a few tall blocks of flats in the suburbs, the sky-line of Prague is still the same. The landmarks were all there, from the famous picture view of the castle to the maze on the hill above, with its distorting mirrors and the enormous panoramic painting of an engagement on the Charles Bridge during the Thirty Years War, a faint pall of smoke still rising from the battle scene. While industry may transform countryside out of recognition, the face of an old town remains essentially the same.

The landmarks were all there, and so were the cafés, restaurants and wine cellars, some of them with the same waiters as twenty years ago. As the place itself was becoming more and more familiar, so were the people. They had been through many years of Stalinism and of its curious Czech extension. They had witnessed public clowning passing under the name of politics; they had been the target of irrelevant propaganda; their lives had been marred by civil insecurity, fear, and the threat of greater horror to come. From all that they have emerged remarkably unscathed.

The impression of my first walk down Václavské náměstí gradually disappeared. It may have been caused by the drifting dust, by the hurrying, dense, self-absorbed crowd. News of the movements of Russian troops in East Germany and Hungary had begun reaching Prague from western sources. At the lowest level, whispered propaganda had not added to the gaiety of the nation; insinuating as it did that the old leaders of the Communist Party had engineered the whole crisis in order to find out who would say what, so that their opponents would declare themselves and be stamped out. 'Vengeance will come down on them like a load of bricks,' I was told while having a glass of beer.

In a way, I shared the return to self-confidence, the gradual improvement in their mood, with the people of Prague. The town and its people became familiar, I recognized their usual, gentle, vulgar language just at the point when I was afraid that we might have lost contact for ever. The Soviet troops apparently ended their manoeuvres and started withdrawing to their stations. The new leaders of the Communist Party were able to gain the trust of the people, and engage their interest by providing them with an unlimited amount of hard information.

Throughout my stay in Prague, I had to get up early in the morning in order to get the day's newspapers. *Rudé Právo*, the Communist Party organ, and *Práce*, the trade unions' paper, were usually available at the stall outside the hotel before eight o'clock, but for *Mladá Fronta*, the youth organization's paper, I had to travel down to the centre of the town and quite often, in the first few days, in vain. Soon I located a stall near the National Theatre, where *Mladá Fronta* was available. The difficulty of getting the daily papers imposed a routine on one's days; having got hold of them I did the morning's work on them at Slavie, the very serviceable café on the corner opposite the National Theatre. Later on in the day it was impossible to work there. Its long, L-shaped room filled with people and with a steady cocktail-party noise. Excitement was its keynote.

Before the beginning of March 1968 newsagents had been returning bales of papers to their publishers every day. As the process of reform gathered speed, interest in politics increased, and so did the sales of newspapers. The rewards of courage and openness were high. Before its closure in October 1967 the writers' weekly *Literární Noviny* was printing 160,000 copies. It was a big edition, and the newspaper owed its success to its fearlessness in the face of the censorship, and its occasional brisk reporting on the social scene. When it resumed publication on 1 March 1968 under the new name *Literární Listy* it had to print 260,000 copies. In Prague, it was unobtainable anywhere outside the town centre.

The two reliable standbys of men's daily conversation – football and women – were almost completely pushed out of circulation by politics. A taxi-driver said that 'Nobody talks about football at my local any longer', and he added that he himself hardly ever read the back, i.e. the sports page of his newspaper, the only part he had had any use for before politics claimed his undivided attention.

I came to enjoy Prague taxi-drivers' conversation, and spent much of my time in cabs. Not that they were easy to get hold of. Reform meant two things for the eight hundred taxi-drivers. Firstly, they wanted to do away with the flat rate they had to pay for every kilometre to their employer, the town transport corporation, whether their car was occupied or not. The system meant that they could lose at night the money they had made during the day, if they were unlucky and picked up a fare to one of the remote suburbs. And secondly, they wanted to get rid of their boss. The flat rate system was enforced by him because he was receiving a bonus based on the number of miles run by cars in his care. Apparently a relative of the old Prime Minister, he was fiercely disliked by his men for the way he treated them when they were reported for having refused a fare. One of my drivers had a scar on his neck eight inches long. He had been attacked and robbed one night by two gipsies who had asked him to drive them to some outlying spot. Their arrest and five-year sentence did not placate the driver: 'They nearly cut my bloody head off for five hundred crowns.' He drove them only because he knew that, if he refused, they would report him. He would have been fired on the spot. Freedom for Prague taxi-drivers therefore meant the freedom to turn down a fare. They used it to the full. On several occasions, for hours on end, not a single taxi was to be seen anywhere, because the drivers were attending a meeting. They got rid of their boss. A few of them had a picture of President Masaryk stuck to the dashboard.

On Palm Sunday I got up early as usual, bought the newspapers, and drove up to Vítkov, the hill beyond the goods yard and railway stations, in the east of the town. The monumentally unattractive building on the top, with tall, narrow windows like unintentional gaps in the expanse of the white walls, with an enormous equestrian statue outside it facing the town, was built between the wars to commemorate the country's independence. Now it serves as a mausoleum for dead communist leaders. A broad flight of stairs leads down into a large hall. At its far end there is a black screen; in the middle, about a dozen brown marble sarcophagi. Only three of them are filled; by Klement Gottwald, who took the Presidency over from Beneš in 1948 and who died soon after having attended Stalin's funeral in Moscow; his successor Antonín Zápotocký, the son of one of the founders of the Social

Democrat party, who died in 1957; and Václav Kopecký, the Minister of Propaganda and Information, the son of the owner of a famous marionette theatre, who died in 1961. Lesser communist luminaries are buried in the white marble coffins alongside the walls; again, most of them are empty. Julius Fučík, a journalist who became the object of a minor but influential cult after the war, is buried in one of the corners of the hall. Four empty black sarcophagi are in a smaller hall below the staircase. There are places in the walls reserved for writers, and smaller ones for party functionaries. Only a few of them are filled as yet.

The architectural defects of the interior, the pointless waste of space and the confusion of levels, the attempt at strict hierarchy of the dead, the whole nonconformist drabness of the largely uninhabited necropolis produces an irritating effect. It is reflected in the visitors' book. American communists, for some unknown reason, write in French, about how much they have been impressed. Visitors from West Berlin write about their wall. The book contains reflections, in many languages, on the impermanence of all forms of human endeavour. Only the sentiments expressed by the Russians are correct.

I drove down the hill, past the wasteland of goods yards and railway tracks, across the town centre and the river, up to the castle and the cathedral. The people attending mass filled the large Gothic nave; incense was being used, for the first time in many years. At the entrance to the cathedral there was a desk, with sheets of paper piled up on it. An old woman, holding a biro, stood nearby. People were signing a petition for religious freedom and the re-introduction of religious instruction into schools.

Yet there was no solemnity in the air in those days, no remote rumble of a revolutionary storm. Even the guards at the castle gate wore sun glasses above their submachine guns. The notice 'We do not sell cigars' in the window of the House of Cuban Culture is a reminder to the passer-by that he is in Schwiek's home town, and that the Good Soldier had been trying to get hold of a good smoke. The pompous grimness of the former President Novotný's regime made a contribution to his fall. Like his slightly less grim and more solid predecessor, Klement Gottwald, Novotný, on hundreds of official photographs, ruled the country wisely but unsmilingly, a pipe clenched tight between invisible teeth. It was too much for the Czechs. They had to suffer personality cult without the personality. There is none of Novotný's stiffness in Alexander Dubček's public appearances. He has the tremendous advantage for a politician of being able to look like a very cheerful duck.

The incredulity of the public at the defeat of the well-established bogey was summed up in a story circulating in Prague on my arrival.

Comrade Lion met a rabbit and said to him, 'Comrade Rabbit, you will come and report tomorrow morning, because I want to eat you for breakfast.' 'I shall be there, you can rely on me, Comrade Lion,' said the rabbit.

Then the lion met a zebra and remarked, 'I shall have you for lunch tomorrow, Comrade Zebra.' 'The pleasure will be mine,' was the reply. Then the lion met a mouse. 'Comrade Mouse, I should like to have you for savoury tomorrow evening. Come and report then.'

The mouse looked the lion straight in the eye, and said, 'You go and stuff yourself, you greedy old thing. I must be on my way now.' 'In that case,' said the lion, 'please accept my apologies and I will of course strike you off my menu.'

A tough and surrealist humour pervades the latest plays. At Viola, the literary nightclub next door to the Writers' Union, a small group of professional actors sang and played *The Songs of the People of Prague*. First published as a book for a poetry club, the *Songs*, of nineteenth-century origin, describe, in detail and without sentimentality, the horrible tales of char-women, prostitutes, sales girls, and their relations with officers of the Habsburg Imperial and Royal Army, mostly drunk. At Malostranská Beseda, two large rooms above the archway in a corner of the square, with tables and chairs instead of the dull, uncomfortable rows of seats (only people over six feet tall can appreciate the sheer comfort of that arrangement) a very good amateur company entertained their young audience with two short plays. The first one, *The Theatre of Jára Cimrman*, was an elaborate joke about literary cults. At a symposium, various experts, including the man who discovered him in the first place, piously rambled on about their master, playwright, philosopher, inventor and polymath. Born in Vienna, Cimrman wrote in German yet always regarded himself as a Czech. He came to die in Bohemia because, in his own words, 'it is a place fit for dying in'. Soon after his death the discovery was made, and the Cimrman industry developed. It is that kind of undergraduate joke, that typically begins by chance, and snowballs happily and wildly all through the term. It is carried over into the interval; a small exhibition of treasured Cimrman relics is on show near the bar, including the master's rusty coffee grinder, all meticulously labelled.

The Drama Club – *Činoherní klub* off the Václavské náměstí – has an extensive repertoire of modern plays by Sean O'Casey, Albert Camus, Edward Albee, and a very high reputation for its acting. Judged by Ladislav Smoček's two demanding short plays, *The Maze* and *The Curious Afternoon of Dr Z. Burke*, the reputation is deserved. Man's weakness and his violence are Smoček's favourite subjects. The pointless violence of the young porter at the maze, the demented violence in defence of his miserable room, displayed by the ageing Dr Burke, are carefully dissected. The first night of Václav Havel's new play at the Theatre on the Balustrade was unfortunately cancelled; I went to see instead the film *Closely Observed Trains*, which was given another run at a cinema in the centre of Prague, after the award of an Oscar in America.

Throughout my stay in Prague, the astounding thing was the hunger for information and more information. The scarcity of daily newspapers bore witness to it; late at night, students were doing brisk trade in the centre of town, selling full transcripts of public discussions. As rebellion flickered across the television screen in the lobby of my hotel, the staff, drivers whose taxis stood deserted outside and Czech-speaking guests came to watch it. Public questioning of members of the party, the government, the army, with a few writers thrown in, was the most popular pastime those days. I attended one of the meetings in Kladno, a tough industrial town about twenty miles west of Prague.

I went there with a writer and with a former member of the party praesidium who had been purged in the early 1950s. When we arrived at the working men's club our driver said, 'You tell them what but make it short and sweet.' He was a good-tempered boy, and was glad to see us when we surfaced more than four hours later. The large hall, festive and draped for the occasion, with a platform at its far side, was full of people, and we found getting to the platform difficult. Some six hundred steel workers were expected and at least eight hundred turned up. Most of them were from the Koněv foundry and they had good reasons for a grudge against the planners in Prague.

Their plant had been founded over a hundred years ago, and even today spades are still the most frequently used tools there. The equipment dates back to the leisurely days at the turn of the century; last year, the foundry made a loss of 170 million crowns. The workers suffer because they are employed at an obsolete plant, and are not getting the benefits – holidays, bonuses – they are entitled to. Recently the government had decided to scrap the wasteful Koněv and build a new, modern plant at Dřín, outside Kladno. Shortly before the meeting on 11 April, questions had been asked as to whether the investment was really necessary.

Probably because of the many sources of discontent the party sent a high-powered team to Kladno. On the chairman's right sat Lieutenant-General Patera, who had fought in the Czechoslovak brigade on the eastern front and then, like his commander and now the new President, General Svoboda, ran into a rough patch in the early 1950s. Next to him was Mr Hanzelka, author of immensely popular travel books; on the extreme right Mr Čestmír Císař, former Minister of Education whom President Novotný had sent as the ambassador to Rumania, and then secretary to the central committee of the party. On the chairman's left was Mr Kraus, the deputy chairman of the planning commission, and a young trade union leader. There was another battery of speakers at the second table; I was sitting behind Císař.

On the way to the platform I was given a badge with the works' trade mark; it was pinned, in a much larger edition, to the yellow drapes at the far end of the hall. It is a girl's head, in profile, with a white star above her, against a blue background, and it made clear to me a line in a recent short story about Kladno, that I had not understood: 'the terrible beauty, her hair singed by stars . . .'

Business was done in an orderly way. Slips of paper with the heading 'a contribution to discussion' were handed out to the audience, who wrote their questions on them, addressing them to one of the speakers. From time to time, the organizers of the meeting brought a batch of the slips and distributed them on the platform. I thought I was there as an observer, until slips addressed to 'the English journalist' started arriving on the table in front of me. A wide range of questions were asked. The steel workers wanted to know what would happen to them and their foundry; what was a ministerial salary; what happened to Czech uranium; what kind of a man was Mňačko, the writer who had recently left the country for Israel; whether the Czechs should have fought Hitler in 1938, and not accepted the Munich agreement.

The questions addressed to me concerned the attitude of Britain and America to the most recent developments in Czechoslovakia.

Some workers left for the afternoon shift, others arrived and took their places. The speakers were well supplied with black coffee and mineral water (I was very glad of that, having spent the night before talking to a friend) and with inquiries from the audience. Only one or two speakers droned on in what I assume was the old-fashioned style, their sentences intentionally dull and unilluminated by thought. But most of the politicians on the platform were entirely open – one of them gave the details of the Soviet-Czechoslovak uranium agreement, another the figures of a ministerial salary – Mr Hanzelka and Mr Čísař were excellent, going fast and with good humour through the stacks of inquiries before them.

I was expected back in town at seven o'clock and it was with difficulty that I got away by 7.20. The meeting was still going on. On the way out, I was given some sandwiches and a wrought iron candlestick, made by the workers, and in return I had to sign invitation cards. The meeting was televised later on in the day.

I went to bed early that night, because I had had breakfast at a sausage stall on Václavské náměstí, after a night spent talking to an old schoolfriend. He was the only friend of my youth I saw in Prague, but he, and the mother of one of my school mates, sketched in for me the lives of many of our mutual acquaintances over the past twenty years. I should say straightaway that the majority of them, all of middle class origin, are now doing jobs I would have expected them to have. Doctors, lawyers, university teachers, publishers: most of my friends who had been students at Prague University after the war have finished their courses. Their drop-out rate was not higher than the sixteen per cent usual in this country. Their parents may have lost their businesses, their money and houses and a few of them have died of the shock. There can be no doubt that some members of the old generation are irreconcilable, and that their lives have been deflected and damaged beyond repair. A simple list of the landmarks in their lives should suffice. Born around the turn of the century, they have seen, in 1918, the break-up of the Habsburg Empire, and the establishment of the Czechoslovak Republic; in 1929 the economic slump; in 1939 the destruction of Czechoslovakia by Hitler, and her reconstruction in 1945; the take-over of power by the Communist Party in 1948.

Their children, now the middle generation, had to come to terms with the political situation after 1948. I think they have done so successfully. Of the people I know, one or two may have joined the Communist Party for the sake of their careers, and this was disapproved of, at the time, by their friends, whatever their political conviction. Otherwise, I did not come across much bitterness, arising out of loss of property or prospects. The few boys I knew – they were the exceptions – who were meant to take over their fathers' businesses, and who did not go to the university, have done on the whole badly. One of them, who has I think suffered more than any other of my friends because of the political development of his country, has had a chequered career of unskilled labour, taxi-driving – the best job he has had so far – and mining. But even he has done what he wanted to do, in a way. When he lived at his parents' large house in the suburbs, he told me he would like to have a small flat in the centre of the town. He has got one now.

The survival and growth of professional, technical and artistic intelligentsia provides one of the principal clues to the present developments in Czechoslovakia. Those men and women of the middle generation, whether party members or not, have watched closely, over the past two decades, the flaws of their political and economic system. They may have been personally affected by them but they bear no bitterness, they harbour no cramping retrospective fury. For some time now they have tried working out the necessary improvements. Those plans have run into stiff opposition. The crisis began more than a year ago and is still (May 1968) far from concluded.

2. The Novotný System

Antonín Novotný, the former President of Czechoslovakia and first secretary of the Communist Party, is a dedicated man. Nobody has ever questioned his devotion to the party.

Born on 10 December 1904 at Letňany, a small village near Prague, Novotný was the son of a bricklayer. After he had spent the basic nine years at school he was apprenticed to a locksmith. Always a serious boy, he never got involved in fights. He was reserved, and seemed to have little in common with his brother and two sisters. He became a member of the Communist Party soon after its foundation in 1920. In 1930, at the age of twenty-five, he reached a position of importance in the organization; he became the chairman of the committee in Karlín, a working-class district in Prague. In 1935 he was elected a member of the committee of the Prague organization, and in March 1937 became its secretary. After the outbreak of the war Novotný worked at the armaments factory at Letňany (his brother was employed there still recently), and as a member of the illegal communist organization. Arrested by the Gestapo in September 1941 he spent most of the war at the Mauthausen concentration camp.

When he returned to Prague in the spring of 1945, Novotný began to consolidate his position in the party hierarchy as the leading secretary of the Prague district organization. It was an important post in the key district. Novotný was then forty-one years old, and the future before him and the party was bright. The party commanded a lot of political goodwill in Czechoslovakia, and ran the largest political organization. Its chairman, from 1946 the Prime Minister, Klement Gottwald, indicated from time to time that there existed a specifically 'Czechoslovak way to socialism'.

Nevertheless, in February 1948, the Communist Party made a successful bid for absolute power in the state. (For a discussion of the possible reasons for that step see below, page 135.) It entrenched itself and its men in positions of power, and started exchanging goodwill for offices in the state. The acquisition of more and more power was stimulated by the desire for absolute control. There was to be, after all, no special Czechoslovak way to socialism. The party leaders decided to follow the Soviet pattern.

Immediately after their February victory, the central committee of the party decided to launch a massive recruitment drive. The party, with 1,409,661 members, was to reach the two million figure. By the end of August 1948, membership had shot up to 2,664,838. Novotný carried out a vigorous recruitment drive in his own district. Party membership was on offer, indiscriminately, in Prague. It was often accepted, out of fear or for the sake of opportunity. When, for instance, a party official with enrolment forms visited the accounting department of a Prague municipal enterprise, only eleven out of sixty-five white-collar workers turned the offer down. The party, and especially its important metropolitan district, became cluttered up by a lot of 'radishes' of contemporary slang: members who were red on the outside, white inside.

After the forced swelling of the ranks of members in 1948, the purges were the next important event in the life of the party. (They are discussed, in connexion with the rehabilitation of former political prisoners, below, page 138.) The first communists lost their offices, and were imprisoned, towards the end of 1949. The party was coming under Stalin's influence: some of its leaders welcomed the new development, and based their careers upon its promotion. The first security 'experts' arrived from Moscow: the establishment of the

Ministry of State Security was announced in May 1950. Antonín Novotný did not yet belong among the leaders of the party, but became one of them during the first wave of arrests. He was appointed one of the six secretaries of the central committee in September 1951; Rudolf Slánský, the secretary general, was arrested on 27 November 1951 and removed from the praesidium of the party on 6 December. Novotný replaced Slánský in the praesidium on the same day. He put himself at the disposal of Stalin's and Beria's experts who came to Prague to supervise the purges. In 1967, when he was fighting for his political life, Novotný must have wished that the words in the official history of the party (*Dějiny Komunistické Strany Československé*, Prague, 1961) had never been written: 'His rich revolutionary experience meant a considerable contribution to the party leadership. The Prague district organization – the biggest one in the Republic – was among those which combated the anti-party activities of Slánský most successfully.'

In March 1953 Klement Gottwald, the President of the Republic and chairman of the party, headed the official Czechoslovak delegation to Stalin's funeral in Moscow. Three days after his return to Prague, Gottwald died. Antonín Novotný became a member of the 'interment committee', and then one of the pall bearers of the dead leader. After a few months when he was in charge of the secretariat of the central committee of the party, Novotný emerged, as the first secretary, at the top of the party hierarchy. It was a new position which obliterated the distinction between the two old posts of party chairman and secretary general.

Though the party gave him the solid foundation of power, Novotný followed Gottwald's example and built up a parallel position for himself in the state. He became a deputy Prime Minister in 1953, and President in 1957. In that year Novotný received the ultimate proof of his greatness: a mountain of the Tyan-Shan range in the Kirgiz Soviet Republic was named after him. One of the main features of the Novotný system was the way the party merged into the state and the state into the party, aggravating each other's faults.

There is evidence, in thousands of his public pronouncements and photographs, that Novotný was deeply impressed by the example of the Soviet leaders. For a long time after Stalin's death, Novotný shaped his public *persona* after the example of the late dictator. It was not an easy task for Novotný. His was a slight, lightweight personality, just capable of supporting one of Stalin's pipes. He certainly could not have got away with one of Stalin's more dramatic public appearances, such as, say, the arrival at the Tempelhof airport, in the midst of the Berlin rubble, in a white Marshal's uniform. The Czechs therefore had to put up with a personality cult which was grim, but not at all grand. When Khrushchev established himself as the undisputed leader in Moscow, Novotný made a few comic attempts at being folksy: but he was more used to the imitation of Stalin's ways. The words that the Soviet Union and its leaders were the best 'teachers' the Czechs and Slovaks have ever had were not an empty phrase for Novotný. There was occasionally such a lack of independence in his actions that it must have amazed the Russians themselves.

Novotný was unlikeable and unpopular, yet he became immensely powerful. Though of working-class origin, he was not, like his predecessor, Klement Gottwald, a workers' leader. He had been present at the foundation of the party as a young man: yet Novotný was not a revolutionary. He had little experience of revolutionary action and of direct political contact with the workers. Novotný's career skipped one stage in the development of European communism in this century: he became a bureaucrat without ever having been a revolutionary. His advance up the party hierarchy was due to dedicated administrative work and to always toeing the party line: to the conformity of a bureaucrat. He possessed dull qualities at a time when they were at a premium. There was a lot of administrative work to be done, and no time for the asking of political questions.

The preoccupations of an earlier era, of politicians like Disraeli or Lenin, Otto Bauer or Thomas Masaryk, who, apart from exercising political power, reflected on its nature, its uses and its limitations, had no place in the thinking of Novotný and his friends. They regarded themselves, at best, as the mechanics of power. For them, all political problems could be reduced to problems of technical manipulation. Their language belonged to the draughtsman's office or the factory floor. When the party leaders wanted to activate the members who, in their turn, set the non-party members into motion, they saw the process as being regulated by levers and transmission belts, the nuts and bolts of a vast blue-print in action.

Novotný was an *apparatchik*, an organization man, who achieved the absolute control of his organization. Many of his contemporaries' political careers had been sidetracked or cut short because a political preference took them too far away from the party line, or because they could not stand the boredom of routine administrative work. Novotný suffered from no such disadvantages. He was just intelligent enough to master the structure and the working of the organization.

From the day Novotný reached the top of the party hierarchy, he never let the day-to-day control of its work slip from his grasp. He was in continuous touch with the many top offices of the party. Even his enemies could not deny Novotný's intimate knowledge of the party apparatus and his skill at manipulating it.

Novotný took care to surround himself by men personally loyal to him. He controlled all the key appointments, the 'cadre policy' in the party and the state. He used a combination of patronage and threat to make his own position unassailable. Party discipline became a fetish and was raised to a martial standard. No dissenting opinions were tolerated:

whenever brave or foolish men expressed them they were in effect resigning their posts or at least jeopardizing their prospects of future advancement. Labels for dissenting opinions were at hand: revisionism, liberalism, bourgeois nationalism, radicalism. When labels ran out, accusations of 'anti-party opposition' or 'anti-socialism' did instead. When a few party members met privately they knew that they were running the risk of being described, or even prosecuted, as a 'fraction'. On one occasion Novotný called a speech by one of his comrades 'disorienting'. The vague, accusing word travelled down the party hierarchy, destroying a political reputation. (Ota Šik in *Kultúrni Noviny*, 29 March 1968.)

It took Novotný some four years to consolidate his position in the party and the state. Klement Gottwald lay, at the time, in an open coffin at the Vítkov mausoleum, dressed in a general's uniform and illuminated by a pink glow. But there were no skilled embalmers in town, and the exhibition did not last long. A gigantic statue of Stalin was erected, and loomed for several years from its pedestal high over Prague. When it was removed, after Khrushchev's speech to the twentieth party congress in 1956, and the government did not accept a West German firm's offer for its considerable scrap metal value, the Czechs were shocked by the waste. The ironic thing was that Novotný and his Stalinist system were firmly established by the time of the disappearance of Stalin's statue.

Novotný's system remained in good running order for almost ten years. It made it both possible and necessary for him to by-pass the central committee. In his party, there was little place for a large consultative body. The new members of of the committee took some time finding out what were its functions. They were usually content, as Novotný's appointments, when they discovered that it was a decorative institution of consent. Power lay in the praesidium, its ten members all hand-picked Novotný men.

Such concentration of power had certain practical disadvantages. Novotný surrounded himself by men similar to himself, who had risen through the party organization. The only difference between them and Novotný was that they were less powerful, and depended on him. He rarely sought or received expert advice: when he did, it was of low quality. The praesidium never delegated any of its immense authority, and Novotný and his comrades found themselves faced with a tremendous amount of work, much of it detailed and unimportant. Cabinet ministers and highly placed executives in industry became used to the system, and relied on Novotný and the praesidium to make their decisions for them. This reliance imposed an enormous burden on Novotný and his praesidium, and destroyed personal initiative at lower levels.

On one occasion a member of the praesidium came into a sharp conflict with Novotný. Rudolf Barák, Minister of Interior from 1954 to 1962 became, in 1956, the head of the party commission that inquired into the political trials in the years 1950–54. It reported on its findings to the party leadership in 1957. Two years later, after a serious illness, Barák started to quarrel with Novotný. (*Kultúrni Noviny*, 5 April 1968.) He attacked Novotný's position of power, and advocated a division of his party and state functions. Having failed to rally enough support for his plan in the praesidium, Barák apparently wrote, confidentially, to Khrushchev. He linked Czechoslovakia's economic difficulties with the slow, indecisive liquidation of the cult of personality, and hinted that a few members of the praesidium had taken part in the preparation and organization of the political trials. Khrushchev sent Barák's letter to Novotný. (Supplement to *Svědectví*, No. 28, Spring 1966.) The struggle in the praesidium ended by Barák's arrest. In 1962, he was sentenced to fifteen years for embezzlement and blamed, inside the party, for a misleading, useless report on the political trials.

Barák was twice defeated. He lost in a straight fight with Novotný and then served as a scapegoat. He was a victim of the way the first secretary used people. An unpopular public measure; a trial balloon; a sensitive task inside the party. Novotný saved his face every time. He was fortunate. There was never a shortage of volunteers.

Yet Barák was quite right if he maintained that the process of de-Stalinization was very slow in Czechoslovakia. Novotný helped to carry Stalin's influence beyond the dictator's grave. Stalin's statue was about the only relic of the past to disappear. But Khrushchev and the Russian leaders had no cause to object.

Novotný listened to Khrushchev's famous speech in Moscow in 1956. After his return to Prague, excerpts from it were circulated in a small pamphlet, intended for the eyes of the high party officials only. But after the disturbances in Poland and the revolution in Hungary, the calm in Prague must have looked especially pleasing from Moscow. The tanks in Budapest had to be followed by aid. Perhaps for the first time since the war, a communist country in Europe proved, to Russia, an economic liability. There were good reasons why the Russians were glad of having a man like Novotný in charge in Prague. Utterly loyal to Moscow, he knew how to keep his countrymen in place. Even the methods he used could be turned to Moscow's advantage. In doing away with some of the worst rigidities of Stalinism, Khrushchev was showing the way to communists in power everywhere, including Czechoslovakia.

Novotný genuinely admired Khrushchev and was much affected by his fall in October 1964. It came a few weeks after the two men had spent a long holiday together at a Slovak spa. Novotný, as soon as he got to know of Khrushchev's fall, sent a telegram to the new Soviet leaders. It said how sorry the Czechs were about Khrushchev's misfortune. It was one of the few tactical errors in Novotný's career.

For a long time, Novotný's regime presented a solid, self-satisfied front to the outside world. The President gave a few interviews to western correspondents, in which dullness and guile were blended in equal proportions. A drab and unexciting place to visit, Czechoslovakia appeared well integrated in the Soviet diplomatic and economic network. Nobody ever stepped out of line. The flaws and weaknesses in Novotný's system were revealed only when he started fighting for his political life.

The struggle began in earnest early in the spring of 1967. The economy, freedom of expression, and Slovakia became the main issues involved. Jiří Hendrych, a member of the praesidium, was Novotný's chief trouble-shooter that year. They had spent the war years together in Mauthausen: they both became central committee secretaries in September 1951. Novotný was prepared to sacrifice Hendrych in the same way he had sacrificed Barák.

At the central committee meeting on 8 February 1967 Hendrych approved the proposals for far-reaching economic reforms, and at the same time recommended the old, restrictive policy for the arts. It was a bad speech, one paragraph contradicting another, with a wide crack running across its overall concept. Hendrych, reflecting Novotný's views, believed that the new economic practice could go hand in hand with the old cultural policy. An economy rigidly planned from the centre, political terror, and strict control and uniformity of all the means of mass communications were the Stalinist trinity. Hendrych spoke as if one whole part could be removed without the others being in the least affected. In May 1967 the central committee again considered the country's economy. Wasteful uses of labour, the large volume of unfinished capital construction, a production not sufficiently geared to the requirements of foreign trade, came under criticism. Capital investment for the year 1967 was to be cut by 1,000 million crowns (the official exchange rate at the time was 20 crowns to £1) and credit policy stiffened. The economic situation was disastrous, and Novotný had had to seek, and accept, outside advice.

But he gave way to pressure only when he absolutely had to. A few days after the meeting of the central committee, on 18 May 1967, a significant incident took place in the National Assembly. Jaroslav Pružinec, a young communist deputy from Pilsen, a bricklayer by occupation, protested, on behalf of a group of twenty-one members, against several new Czechoslovak films. The protests referred to Věra Chytilová's *Daisies*, Jan Němec's *Of Feasts and Guests* and to other films. Addressing various ministers, Pružinec asked,

How much longer will those artists go on poisoning the lives of honest working people, how much longer will they tread our socialist progress into the mud, how much longer will they go on wrecking the nerves of the workers and the peasants? Anyway, what kind of democracy are you trying to introduce? Why do you think we have the frontier guard, fulfilling its combat task of protecting us against the external enemy, while we, comrades Ministers of Defence and Finance, are paying large sums of money to our internal enemy? We let them, comrade Minister of Agriculture, tread in and destroy the fruits of our labour. [IV. *Sjezd Svazu čs. Spisovatelů*, Prague, 1968, page 136]

The film makers and, with them, all the Czech intellectuals were meant to take the hint. They had gone too far, against the interests of the broad masses of the people. There were nasty, threatening undertones in the speech delivered to the Assembly. Mr Pružinec's curious, threatening assault on the intellectuals was merely an extension of Novotný's way of running the economy.

According to official doctrine, the state was based on a union of the workers, the peasants and the intelligentsia (the 'workers of the brain', in the official parlance). Over the years, however, the objective of Novotný's system was to create, and maintain, a corporate society, a modern variation on medieval guilds. (cf. Karel Kosík's series of articles in *Literární Listy*, starting on 11 April 1968.) The three classes became in fact more and more isolated from each other. The factories were reserved for the workers, the fields for the peasants, the libraries for the intellectuals. The workers, isolated from the intellectuals, stopped playing any political role whatsoever. The peasants disappeared from political life. The nation was on the way to 'becoming Czech-speaking consumers of wheat and producers of steel'. The bureaucracy became the leading class, providing the only link among the three officially recognized classes. It alone possessed the necessary overall information, and was able to run the system. Early on in his life at the top, in March 1956, Novotný told the central committee that 'workers in justice and security' had become 'the main instruments of class struggle'. The working class was deprived of its historic mission: the top bureaucrat had no need to parade as a Marxist revolutionary.

The purpose, therefore, of Pružinec's inquiry to the National Assembly in May 1967 was to sow distrust between the intellectuals and the workers, and keep them divided. Later, when hard pushed, Novotný himself came down on the factory floor, and warned the workers against a sinister 'dictatorship of the intellectuals, in which they, the workers, would reenter their old bondage'.

While new divisions were created in the nation in the Novotný era, an old one was being healed. After 1948, there had existed the distinction between the people inside and outside the Communist Party. The outsiders were in the majority. (In 1949, for instance, the party had 2,311,066 members: the census of 1950 gave the total population of Czechoslovakia at 12,464,384.) People outside the party thought of its members as a united and well-informed collective, able to participate in the making of important decisions. Party members were not allowed to discuss party affairs (this eventually came to mean every political issue) with non-members. Yet the non-communists' view of the communists soon became out of date. Inside the party, the rank-and-file accepted their leaders as being omniscient and omnipotent. The party leaders, in return, took a low view of their comrades' maturity, and assumed that they were incapable of taking decisions. In this way, the distinction between the communists and the non-communists disappeared. Only the manipulators, the 'technicians of power', and the masses remained. Each group regarded the other with a blank, anonymous face. The manipulators had absolute power, without having accepted absolute responsibility.

Since the spring of 1967, however, not a single month passed without Novotný's system coming under a severe test. On 10 June 1967 Prague, following the Soviet Union's lead, broke off relations with Israel. Czechoslovakia had been fully committed in the Middle East since 1955. In that year the Czechs signed their first agreement on arms deliveries to Egypt. Arms deals with Syria and the United Arab Republic followed; military delegations were exchanged; Egyptian pilots were trained in Czechoslovakia.

The diplomatic move on 10 June 1967 followed hard on the emergency meeting of communist leaders – Novotný and Lenárt, the Prime Minister, were present – in Moscow the day before. On 11 June, Novotný made his third speech, since the beginning of the Middle Eastern crisis, charging Israel with aggression. The Foreign Ministry chimed in. On 25 May 1967 it had accused Israel of having created tension in the Middle East, in collusion with 'imperialist circles directly connected with oil monopolies'; on 6 June, the Ministry stated that Israel had started hostilities the day before, thereby committing aggression against the United Arab Republic.

The official policy was unpopular, not only inside the small Jewish community in Czechoslovakia. The customary phrases about imperialism, with antisemitic undertones, were too reminiscent of the grim years of the early 1950s, when the trials against Slánský and others were being prepared. The country was then living in a state of siege: the people, suspicious and divided against themselves, were cut off from the outside world. Listening to the official propaganda in the summer of 1967, it may have occurred to many Czechs and Slovaks that nothing much had changed in the past fifteen years. And then, the swift and absolute failure of Arab arms did not rally the people behind their government's policy in the Middle East.

3. The State of the Writers' Union

Between 27 and 29 June the fourth congress of Czechoslovak writers took place in Prague. Some four hundred writers turned up, in addition to the Ministers of Education and of Culture and Information, and a party delegation led, as usual, by Jiří Hendrych. Novotný came nowhere near the large assembly hall of the Ministry of Transport, where the congress was taking place. It was an almost exclusively Czech occasion. The Slovak writers had fought their own fights, and they did not want any help from Prague.

The Czechs have never had many writers who wrote only to entertain. Politics and literature had gone hand in hand in their tradition, and all their major literary figures kept on crossing the borderline between writing and politics. Their language, their very nationality stood in question early in the nineteenth century. Czech was a dialect spoken almost exclusively in the countryside, it was a peasant's tongue, stunted and clumsy. The rising middle class, the sons and daughters of the peasant migrants to towns, had a straightforward choice before them. They could either merge with their German environment or maintain their Czech individuality. They made the latter choice. Their writers played the leading role in the building up of their national consciousness as much as of their language. In May 1917 the writers' manifesto signed the death warrant of the Habsburg Empire.

Before the outbreak of the Second World War some of the best-known writers were members or sympathizers of the Communist Party and contributors to its daily *Rudé Právo*. Ivan Olbracht, Marie Majerová, Josef Hora were on the newspaper's staff: Jiří Wolker, Helena Malířová, Vítězslav Nezval, Vladimír Vančura wrote for it. Zdeněk Nejedlý, the biographer of Smetana and Masaryk (only of their early years: Nejedlý had a passion for detail) who after the war held high government posts, was the music critic on the party newspaper. He often quarrelled with the editors of *Rudé Právo*. When he thought that they were being too sentimental in their literary policy, he told them that 'a sentimental revolutionary is a disgusting sight'.

'The language of communism is hard,' Karel Čapek wrote in his essay *Why I Am Not a Communist* in 1924, 'it is not sentimental ... only a cad and a demagogue are not sentimental. Without sentimental reasons you will not pass a glass of water to another human being.' What Čapek disliked most about communism was its 'peculiar gloom'. He took the side of the poor ('shake the world and then go and have a look who is buried under the rubble'), but he maintained that

in spite of the lies in the party programme no proletarian culture exists: we have today no folk culture or religious culture: the middle, so-called intelligent class preserves what is left of cultural values. If the proletariat claimed its share in this tradition, if it said: good, I shall take over the present world with all its values, we could shake hands and try it. But if communism pushes forward and dismisses the so-called bourgeois culture as unnecessary junk, then goodbye ...

Čapek accused the communists of exploiting the poor. There was to be no relief for them before the dawn of the glorious revolution.

I am especially sorry for the proletarians, who are cut off from the rest of the educated world without being given any substitute other than the prospect of the pleasures of the revolution. Communism stands as a barrier between them and the world. You, communist intellectuals, stand, holding brightly coloured shields, between them and everything that has been made ready for them, the new arrivals.

Later, Karel Čapek opposed Hitler's dictatorship. He died in 1939 before the Germans could lay their hands on him. His brother, Josef Čapek, the painter and writer, died in a concentration camp, and so did many distinguished communist writers and intellectuals.

In 1948, the new communist government expected a lot from its authors. Their political commitment was taken for granted, and so was their willingness to help the party build a new kind of political and social system. Most of the new rulers of Czechoslovakia had been party functionaries before 1939 and had spent the war either in Moscow or in Nazi concentration camps. They overestimated and misunderstood the power of writing – any kind of writing – to inform and influence the actions of men. A novelist who wrote about, say, the countryside was expected to make a positive contribution to the implementation of the government's agricultural policy. He was required to trespass on the territory in this case covered by specialized agricultural journals. Literature in all its forms, from works of imagination down to trade magazines, suffered accordingly. The writers, the heart and the brain of the nation, were required to become unfeeling, unthinking instruments of the policy of the government. In the eyes of the people, the writers sank even lower than that. An author who spent some weeks in a hospital bed next to a talkative patient with an interest in politics, was told by a nurse, as he was leaving the hospital, 'We were afraid when they put you in that room. Mr K is so careless in his speech, and we were afraid that you would denounce him to the police.' When he asked the nurse why, she replied, 'We looked it up in your identity card, and you gave your occupation as "writer".' The price paid by the Czech writers for their political involvement was high, but they would have it no other way. They had made a place for themselves at the very centre of their society, instead of living, like writers in the West do, as more or less comfortable exiles on their society's margins.

It was said in Prague that the party had found planning literature and the arts easier than planning the economy. Hendrych's speech to the central committee in February 1967 confirmed that view. Persuasion and compulsion, in all the ways in which a totalitarian state uses them, were put to work among the writers and the artists. They either supported the current cultural line or their work did not see the light of day.

For the writers, a narrow interpretation of social utility obtained, and an almost inhuman piety was required of them. Josef Škvorecký's novel *The Cowards* caused the biggest literary scandal of the 1950s because its few references to the Red Army did not take the accepted form of adulation. In painting and sculpture, any kind of abstraction or surrealism was ruled out. In that regard the tastes of Stalin and Hitler were similar, and in both cases, they were thoroughly imposed. In the 1950s, in the same way as during the Nazi occupation, jazz became an underground cult of the young. The greatest enemies of a Goebbels or a Zhdanov were Louis Armstrong, Stan Kenton and a whole army of jazz musicians and their followers. They fought, and in many cases won, the war for the soul of east European youth. While Khachaturian and many lesser men preached against the hot gospel in solemn pronouncements, the 'Czechoslovak Washboard Beaters' or the 'Prague City Stompers' blew and stomped away in the umbrageous semi-legality of Prague cellars. The author of *The Cowards* was then asked to join the party, by a very pretty girl whom he liked to tease. He renounced the party, and probably the girl as well, on the grounds that the party was against jazz and Hemingway. (*Literární Listy*, 18 April 1968.) An institutionalized and frequently bogus kind of folklorism – the regional ensembles that sung and danced – was the only contribution of that policy to the cultural scene.

Soon after the communist take-over of power in 1948 a lot of people in official positions had views on what kind of books were needed, what kind of pictures were the most pleasing, what kind of music was the most melodious, which films were the most valuable. Doubtless the Ministry of Culture and Information tried out some of those views in practice. The Ministry was, after all, full of practising artists. Some of them may have regarded their Ministry jobs as sinecures, and visited their offices only when it rained outside; others could not keep up the high tone of their new posts indefinitely. Over the years 'direction of the arts and literature' became more and more restrictive. The officials found it easier to have views on what should not be written, painted, etc., and the system came more and more to rely on censorship.

For many weeks after the peaceful revolution early in 1968, Prague newspapers carried articles that had been censored in the past two years. Before the closure of the *Literární Noviny* in the autumn of 1967, the editor had to have a replacement article ready for every slightly questionable piece. Week after week, he was editing two newspapers instead of one. The writers learned their lessons and wrote allegories, historical satire, fables to fox the censor. They knew that a refusal by one paper by no means ended an article's useful life. The censor's inability to grasp the meaning of the text before him occasionally loosened the system, which was based on preventive, preliminary censorship and run by the Central Publicity Administration in the Ministry of the Interior. For almost twenty years publishers had to have manuscripts scrutinized by the censors before they could be taken to the printers. Daily newspapers had resident censors attached to them.

It is not a situation the Czechs have been used to. The Habsburg Imperial law of 4 March 1849 provided for freedom of expression. Though it was often disregarded and sometimes suspended, the December constitution of 1867 gave freedom to the press once and for all. In the first Czechoslovak Republic the right of the police censor to issue a confiscation order was used occasionally, and *Rudé Právo*, the communist daily, probably suffered more than any other paper, especially in the early 1930s. But preliminary censorship was unknown between the years 1918 and 1938.

Someone with a fine sense of irony must have fixed the date for the passing of the new Czechoslovak press law for 1967, on the centenary of the original Habsburg law. It granted the right to publish only to organizations and not to individuals, and it demanded registration of the proposed periodical by the Ministry of Culture. It could refuse registration if 'the publication of the periodical is not secure in advance technically, financially and economically, or if the application did not guarantee that the periodical would 'fulfil its social mission'. Paragraph 17 of the press law stated that 'if the content of the information runs counter to the interests of society the Central Publicity Administration will inform the editor and the publisher'. Newspapers were under pressure from two sides: preliminary censorship was supplemented by ideological guidance issued by the Communist Party. This meant that editors received a stream of directives, a practice similar to that on which Dr Goebbels founded his control of the Nazi press. At the writers' conference in June 1967 Ivan Klíma said that:

It is impossible to visualize censorship, a physically existing group of censors, which, over the long years of activity in the midst of a stable society, would not degenerate into a bureaucratic institution, in its turn breeding degeneration and becoming an obstacle to social progress. [*Literární Listy*, 7 March 1968]

The Czechs could find nothing to say in their censors' favour. When Saltykov-Shchedrin, Russia's civil servant and satirist, described, more than a century ago, a censor's spiritual torture, he was at least able to take the reader on a tour of the censor's exquisite flat. His Czech successors had nothing like that to show for their dedicated work.

More forceful means of coercion than censorship were at

hand. In 1952 fifteen writers were sentenced in all to 220 years of imprisonment. By the time amnesty was declared in 1960 and they started being released, they had served some 130 years. The Ministry of Justice 'rehabilitated' them all, but in an underhand way, as if the officials were ashamed of something. For Dr Bedřich Fučík troubles really began when he was set free. (See the interview in *Literární Listy*, 4 April 1968.) The article he wrote about his release, the 'victory of reason and justice', was censored and never appeared. The author was given a tiny pension (pensions granted to older former political prisoners varied between 200 and 400 crowns, just enough to buy a decent pair of shoes, certainly not enough to live on for a month) and he started to negotiate with the Ministry of Justice for compensation. His complaint was that his house having been confiscated, his wife was allowed to live in one half of it, but was charged rent. A sum was agreed on, about a third of the actual amount actually paid out in rent for the author's own house. Then the Ministry started bargaining. The official said that board and lodgings during Dr Fučík's imprisonment had cost the state 300 crowns a month: the author told the man that he had worked when in prison. The representative of the Ministry of Justice replied with impeccable logic: if you were not in prison, you could not earn money there. The author's comment:

You no longer understand, you are ashamed of yourself, you helplessly sign the 'contract' about the compensation, because after so many years you do not find enough confidence in yourself to sue the Ministry of Justice in a court run by the Ministry of Justice. You sign, in the same way that years ago you signed your confession of guilt, and you do it only to be left in peace, peace, peace! You are angry but what's more, you again have the same feeling of humiliation, of the helplessness of the individual confronted by force.

In his interview in April 1968, after he had described his life a few years ago, Dr Fučík refused to talk about the means his interrogators had used to get his 'confession of guilt'.

In a recent essay (*Literární Listy*, 2 May 1968) Miroslav Holub, the scientist and poet, wrote that the 'killing of words precedes the killing of people. Science and literature, two sources of the modern world and modern humanity, are based on the direct and irrevocable relationship between the word and the object.' In the last twenty years 'slaughterhouse conditions' have obtained in regard to words. The main reason for that situation was, according to Holub, that whatever was done, good or bad, was surrounded either by a veil of secrecy or by a strange coyness, which were called, among other things, 'watchfulness' or 'alertness'. Show trials either 'did not exist', or were called 'justice' or 'will of the people'; genetics was called 'bourgeois pseudo-science'; price increases became 'readjustments' of prices; nomination of people to representative bodies was called 'elections'. 'This clowning . . . gave public life the special taste of living in some imaginary country, where the mother tongue was translated into a primitive dialect', a country where 'the general feeling of guilt was spread and multiplied, a guilt derived from knowledge of the dark sides of reality, but which began every time a mouth opened to speak'.

After an experience like that 'many words are dead, many sick, and new words are afflicted by epilepsy'. Holub issued a stern warning against the 'fever of new words' like 'consent', 'we all', 'youth' ,'elections', 'democracy'. They have to be weighed, examined from every side, before they are put into circulation. Anyway, 'democracy' is, according to Holub, a very sick word indeed in the Czech language. Even a simple pronoun like 'we' has fallen sick: '. . . it became feudalized. It does not name, it makes value judgements.'

At the same time as the army of some 70,000 political prisoners was slowly being disbanded, a thaw started cracking the ice-bound literary scene. The Czech and Slovak writers may have felt that they had missed the boat after the twentieth Soviet party congress in 1956, and that the same thing could happen again after the twenty-second congress in 1961. They feared that the comparative freedom their Russian and especially Polish colleagues were then enjoying would never reach Prague or Bratislava. It did, only very much later. In the end it went further than in any other part of eastern Europe.

The future historian may well have to look for the beginnings of the Czechoslovak spring – it is now much more than a thaw – in the editorial offices of the Czech and Slovak newspapers and periodicals. The editors of *Literární Noviny, Kultúrný Život, Mladá Fronta, Host do domu, Plamen* took a lot of calculated risks. They were harassed by the censor but they, in their turn, did not leave the censors in peace. It was not merely a war of verbal attrition. Livings, if not lives, were at stake.

Ladislav Mňačko was the first to break out of the decorous restrictions under which Czechoslovak men of letters lived and worked. His *Belated Reports* (*Opožděné reportáže*) appeared in Bratislava in 1964. First serialized in *Kultúrný Život*, the Slovak writers' newspaper, the book soon sold 300,000 copies that often changed hands at black-market prices. The Czechs were astonished. One of their writers remarked, 'At first my heart almost stopped beating, so unbelievable seemed the daring of the author and his publishers.' (*Literární Noviny*, 19 December 1964; cf. *Survey*, April 1965.) Mňačko's subject was Stalinism and the way it affected the whole society. He saw it not as a conspiracy by a few individuals behind the Kremlin walls, but as a social problem.

Mňačko touched on the question of responsibility, including his own, for Stalinism. He had admired Stalin but then, while working for a newspaper, began to realize the difference, the contradictions, between the private and public faces of that system. The stories of *Belated Reports* were the kind of case histories that a journalist collects; Mňačko gave them a political and moral slant, and was ready to take risks. He described, for instance, how a party functionary, a 'man of vast stupidity', organized a shoddy provincial show trial, in order to camouflage his past blunders. Though some of Mňačko's characters were the customary stereotypes, and he did not press his inquiry far enough, his collection of short stories was a pioneering experiment.

It was neither repeated nor pursued further for a long time. After Milan Kundera submitted the manuscript of his novel *The Joke* (*Žert*) in 1966, its publication was held up because the censor wanted the author to drop a commonly used term for units of national servicemen who were unarmed, and used for heavy labour, because they were regarded as politically unreliable. The censor's explanation was that those units had no existence in law. The appearance of the book in the following year, as well as the publication of Ludvik Vaculík's *Sekyra* (*The Axe*) in 1966, became the major literary events since the end of the war. Both Vaculík and Kundera are in their early forties, they were both born in Moravia, and they have been working journalists. They are members of the Communist Party. Their novels are about men trying to come to terms with their past, the authors in both cases the narrators.

The 'joke' of Kundera's title affects a young man's whole life. A party member and an officer of the university students' union in Prague sent a postcard, in the vacation of the year 1948, to a serious-minded but attractive girl, a first-year student, then undergoing ideological training in the country. (The girl's seriousness like the seriousness of that time 'did not wear a frown but the face of a smile', as everybody who did not visibly enjoy himself was 'at once suspect that he was unhappy about the victory of the working class or, in no way a lesser crime, that he was selfishly immersed in some private sadness'.) The message on the postcard was 'Optimism is the opium of the people! Long live Trotsky!' His comrades at the university took the joke seriously. He was expelled from the party and sent down from the university. He became

politically suspect, did his national service in the mines, stayed
on for a few extra years. After 1956 he succeeded in finishing
his university course and was employed in a scientific institute
in Prague. While working there he met the wife of his former
comrade (their 'marriage a part of party discipline') whom
he held responsible for his dismissal from the party and the
university. Their meeting at the narrator's native town, an
ugly provincial place somewhere in Moravia, and the attempt
to revenge himself by humiliating his comrade's wife form the
framework of the novel.

The atmosphere of the early years of Stalinist Czechoslovakia, of the work in the mines, of the Moravian provincial
town is skilfully evoked; the bitter, wry humour is the author's
own. The contents of a provincial student's locker, a suicide
gone wrong because laxative instead of sleeping tablets were
taken, such descriptions are very comic indeed. But his main
interest is moral, illuminated by and illuminating a detailed
examination of men's motives. It was wrong to misunderstand
an innocent joke so savagely, and it was equally wrong to
have sought revenge for so long. The narrator finds out that
his comrade of many years ago and his wife had separated;
that their marriage, like party discipline, had become something quite different; even inflicting physical punishment on
her did not make sense, because the woman was a masochist.

Reading Kundera's novel soon after its appearance early
in 1967 made one concerned for the author's future. Novotný,
his old guard, their censors all appeared firmly entrenched,
and they were still concerned with 'giving false evidence'.
Ludvík Vaculík's novel *The Axe*, published a few months
before Kundera's, showed the same preoccupations in a different context. Tremendously tightly woven, *Sekyra* has the
texture of a poem rather than a novel.

Kundera's narrator regards himself as a failure, Vaculík's
is an unashamed success. The tension between his Prague,
journalistic present and his Moravian past is strong; he too is

a man who can find himself only by understanding his past. (The last paragraph of the book opens with the sentence, 'I gained a lot thereby: the original, sharp consciousness.') It is more private, less political than the past of Kundera's narrator, but politics keep breaking in. The hero of *The Axe* returns to a countryside that has been totally transformed. He wants to understand the nature of that change and its impact on the people who made and suffered by it.

After the war, his father, a worker, became a local communist functionary. He quarrelled with his relatives and friends, most of them just as poor and stubborn as he was. He suffered by the change perhaps more than they did. Issued with a gun in the early days of collectivization, when party and district officials were often assaulted, he thought of using it against himself rather than against his own people. He was puzzled, towards the end of his life, because his eldest son – the narrator – was not interested in claiming his inheritance, the poor cottage his father had built, which 'had become old before it was finished'.

In one of the last and most powerful chapters of the novel, Vaculík's narrator describes his visit to his uncle's and aunt's cottage nearby. ('Only I myself knew for certain that I was coming on that visit.') The uncle, with whom his father had quarrelled most bitterly about the party's agricultural policies, was 'now a very old man who for long has not been putting together new sentences', only wanted to know whether '. . . you haven't such a hard life like your old dad. Or have you?' His cousin Charles, his slow, peasant strength ill used in short periods of occasional unskilled labour, had achieved an uneasy truce with the world. After a specially profitable job, he bought an expensive piano (the journalist knew he could never afford to do that) and tuned it himself, each of the three strings of a single note differently, one slightly higher, one slightly lower, one true 'especially for the sake of Bach'; he now played Bach, his clumsy fingers 'leaving the keys only when absolutely required elsewhere'. Charles, who did not drink because he wanted to be around when 'they drink themselves into the ditch and that should be soon' had his piano, his fiercely guarded independence. He never complained to the authorities; he did not care for the vulgarity, the dishonesty, the total lack of justice of the period: 'this era favours the stupider half of men. Let it do so, but without me.'

The narrator agreed, even admired his cousin, but knew he could not opt out so easily. He had made his political decision, declared his commitment, in Prague. He was a journalist who knew the 'hard work of writing something that will be published and yet leave a part of my honour untouched'. On one occasion he was sent to investigate a complaint by 'a girl of that rare type, meant to lead a difficult life or worse'. The article upset a lot of local people, the girl killed herself. The doctor who had examined her and then committed perjury when giving evidence to the investigating committee, later explained his deception: 'she was much more of a virgin than those bastards were the elected representatives of the people.'

The girl's father who assaulted the members of the committee without being told of his daughter's death, was put into a lunatic asylum, run by an old psychiatrist who believed in the therapeutic effect of gardening on mental illness. Rapidly, by a few strokes, Vaculík sketched in the psychiatrist's particular madness. He believed that the process of natural selection was not yet complete, and that, while in the past its agent was, say, climate, it is now 'social-psychological pressure'. When asked whether it was his own idea, the psychiatrist said no, that it was a commonly accepted theory in the West, and was spreading from there. Then he added that he abhorred western society, with its faulty contacts between 'the cognition of its own state and the movement towards its regulation'. The psychiatrist's subsequent contribution to Czech thought was his own: 'I should prefer it if we remain a pleasantly backward country. What do you say to that! Russia will survive the crash of the so-called industrial society basically because she has not been fully affected, so that she will be unharmed and spiritually healthy to accept the system that must be born in the crash.'

Vaculík's journalist-narrator got into some trouble for the pains he had taken over the girl. He was ready to defend himself. He did not accept the defence, made on his behalf, that he 'meant well', he did not rely on his impeccably working-class origins. He would have no more of the act of 'self-terrorization' that the party expected of its members: 'That's all the Czech invention is: we terrorize ourselves so democratically that there is no one left to assassinate.'

The appearance of those two books on the literary scene resembled the impact of Janáček's music in the nineteen-twenties. They had in common a certain freshness, a directness as well as the powerful tensions below the surface. They are the most striking examples of the kind of writing that has been appearing more and more frequently in the past two years in Czechoslovakia. It staked out historical landmarks; it healed the relationship 'between the word and the object'; it prepared the ground for political developments. It was fully politically committed.

The examples of free writing that reached the public from time to time received little praise from the party leaders. They may have realized that such works would go on slipping through the censor's net so long as the party had no consistent or positive literary policy. Another attempt was made to formulate one in June 1967, just before the writers were about to meet at their fourth congress. A pamphlet with the inviting title *A Draft for the Activities of the Ministry of Culture and Information* was produced 'for official use only'. It opened with the bold statement that there are two kinds of art, 'art accessible to only a small number of people' and that 'for the broad masses', and the latter kind has the 'chief social significance'. (It seems that the Ministry had tried to put this policy into practice. Vaculík's and Kundera's books appeared in small editions; clubs for 'demanding audiences' were started, showing films not on general release.) The Ministry proposed to 'judge important events in cultural life and evaluate their social significance'. It would try to act as an inspiration to the arts, by taking 'cultural initiative' and adding the sanction of 'demand by the community'. Literary competitions, prizes, a new structure of royalties – echoes of economic reforms – were to be used as further incentives to artistic production.

By the time the writers started arriving at their congress in Prague in the summer of 1967, the rules of their quarrel with the party bureaucracy had been laid down. They wanted their freedom to write what they liked and as they pleased; the party demanded their loyalty, non-interference in political matters, and the occasional use of their skills. But the definitions were loose and the rules too fluid, and the contest came to resemble an all-in wrestling bout. The writers, through their Union, had proved their ability to act as a united interest and pressure group.

Before the opening of the congress, the Union had prepared a paper containing proposals that were to serve as the basis for discussion. It had been drafted with the help of the ideological section of the party, rewritten several times, and still the party leadership did not agree with the draft. It provided not a common platform but the ring in which the fight took place. Trouble was expected, and all the communications media gave the congress minimum publicity.

In the morning of the first day of the congress, 27 June 1967, Milan Kundera spoke. A member of the Union's praesidium, Kundera had taken part in working out the preliminary draft with the ideological section. He knew the layout of the areas of conflict exactly. He made a wide-ranging, important speech.

Years of frustration and thought had gone into its making. Most nations, Kundera said, would take their national existence for granted. The Czechs could not. Their national life had passed too near to death's door for that: they had had, in the nineteenth century, a stark choice before them. They knew that, by becoming Germans, their lives would have been easier, there would have been better opportunities for their children. They knew all about the disadvantages of small nations who, according to Kollár, the Slovak poet, 'think and feel almost only by halves', their civilization being a 'mean and sick thing; it does not live, but only survives, it does not flower but only vegetates, it does not produce trees, only shrubs'. The Czechs made their choice with their eyes wide open. They had to justify it before history.

They could do so, and this had also been known to them, only by getting rid of provincialism. Another nineteenth-century writer and poet, Jan Neruda, wrote that 'we are now assuming the duty to raise our nation to the level of world civilization ...' All the builders of Czech nationality in the nineteenth century knew this. They wanted their people to take their place among the peoples of Europe, of the world. This was the reason why, Kundera said, Czech literature created an unusual type of writer – the translator – a very important, sometimes the leading, literary personality. Such had been the case in the period before the counter-reformation: the Czechs had the first translations of Erasmus in Europe. In the nineteenth century, Jungmann's translation of Milton was built into the very foundations of the revival of the Czech language. Nevertheless, Kundera went on, the Czechs had had their times of wakefulness and times of sleep. They never could take anything for granted, their language, their being a part of Europe.

Then, early in the twentieth century, 'especially in the period between the two world wars, Czech civilization came to, doubtless, the greatest flowering in its history'. The Czechs

now tend to feel nostalgic about that extremely short and
intensive period. Still, in their literature

the lyrical style was dominant, it was only in its beginning and it
needed only time, long, peaceful, and continuous. To interrupt that
development first by the Nazi occupation, then by Stalinism,
almost quarter of a century altogether, to isolate it from the outside
world, to do away with its manifold inner tradition, to reduce it
to the level of barren propaganda, that was a tragedy which threatened to remove the Czech nation, once and for all, to the outer
suburbs of European civilization.

Kundera then went on to demonstrate that while 'life
becomes more and more international' in the second half of
the twentieth century, the 'effectiveness of the languages of the
small nations becomes more and more limited'. They can
therefore be defended only on the ground of their importance,
of the values they created. Pilsner beer is of course also a
value, Kundera said, but it is known everywhere under its
German name, and anyway, it cannot justify the Czechs'
right to their own language. 'The future of the world now
being unified will ruthlessly and justly demand the reckoning
of the national existence which we chose one hundred and
fifty years ago, and it will ask why we chose it.'

Another point the speaker made carefully was that Czech
literature is a plebeian literature, not at all aristocratic. Closely
linked up with the national 'hinterland which strongly echoes
its word' it is also too dependent on its public, on its level of
tolerance and civilization. 'I am sometimes frightened that
our present civilization is losing that European character, that
lay so close to the hearts of the Czech humanists and revival-
ists.'

Kundera was convinced that the future of Czech literature
and the arts depends on the possibility of their free development.

I know that when freedom is mentioned some people get hay
fever and reply that every freedom must have its limits. Of course

every freedom has its limits, given by the state of contemporary knowledge, education, prejudice, etc. Yet no progressive period has ever tried to fix its own limitations! ... Only, in our case, the guarding of frontiers is still regarded as a greater virtue than crossing them.

Though Kundera put his case with great force and skill he let off, towards the end of his speech, some fireworks peculiarly his own. He said he did not like the equation between fascism and Stalinism. Fascism had created a morally simple situation because it left the humanist principles and virtues untouched by being opposed to them. Stalinism on the other hand, the heir of a great humanist movement, retained many of its original attitudes, ideas, slogans. 'To watch such a humanist movement being perverted into something opposite, removing every human virtue, transforming love for humanity into cruelty to people, love for truth into denunciation, opens up tremendous insights into the very foundations of human values and virtues.'

The whole story of the nation, not only of life under Stalinism but also under fascism, its experience of democracy multiplied by the problem of its nationality, all that is the essence of our time. It made the twentieth century into what it is.

This nation has perhaps lived through more in this century than many other nations, and if its genius has been awake, it perhaps even knows more. This knowledge could be used for that liberating crossing of the present frontiers, in the crossing of the present limits of our knowledge of man and of his lot, and in that way give Czech civilization its sense, maturity, greatness.

Do the Czechs know of their opportunity? Will they be allowed to use it? Kundera asked in conclusion. (The speech was printed in full in *Literární Listy*, 21 March 1968.)

After Kundera's challenging survey, Alexander Kliment and Edward Goldstücker discussed the conflict between politics and art; Pavel Kohout attacked the government's policy in the

Middle East. On the second day, A. J. Liehm, the literary critic and historian, contributed a detached analysis of the various types of cultural policies in Europe. In connexion with the renaissance, for instance, Liehm argued that the 'competition of patrons' contributed to the breaking of the cultural policy of the church and of the medieval state. The middle classes of the nineteenth century, who 'democratized the privileges of the aristocracy', gave the artist and writer his freedom but drove him into the market place. Corpses of artists who did not make it in their own time are scattered all over the nineteenth century.

The cultural market was then in the main a minority market, and only the consumers' society of the last twenty years changed the situation. 'In the end liberalism in its own way brought about even the democratization of culture that is really impressive and that often fills us with envy.' Only it promotes, Liehm pointed out, high and low grade goods with equal zest.

The task of the socialist society, as Liehm sees it, is to free culture from the double pressure, the pressure of political power and the pressure of the market place, and then to make it generally available, to make everyone feel the need for it.

Tracing the historical development, Liehm discerned the various faces of culture 'distorted by uniformity'. At present, socialist cultural policy has been through so many disasters that the Czechs tend to idealize the situation in the West. The trouble is that the two pressures, instead of being removed altogether, are turned on and off.

Political pressure should be taken off and the freedom of the writer and the artist should be limited by nothing else but criminal law. The socialist state should provide a material guarantee for culture. Mr Liehm did not explain how the latter aim could be achieved. He pointed out that the Czech cultural market is so small that it could not act as a regulator in any case. He asked the state to cushion the artist and provide material abundance for him, as well as for his public. He said that, in his view, the United States need not necessarily be the first to reach that goal. Even a 'poor and impoverished society, even a society that has paid, and will pay, a disproportionately big tax for its search for a functioning model of socialism', can make the attempt, and make it first.

On the second day of the congress dissenting voices were heard from among the writers themselves. A letter was read out, signed by several writers, Jan Drda and Jarmila Glazarová, well-known novelists of the older generation, among them. It accused some of the speakers of producing an 'atmosphere of nervousness and tension', and some of the speeches as low-level 'politicking'.

The address by Ludvík Vaculík did nothing to cool down the rising temperature. His opening sentence had the authentic Vaculík shape: 'Comrades, I am using this opportunity to tell you what you know anyway, because I should like to add to it a few concrete reminders.' Vaculík chose the most sensitive topic: the problem of political power, in its Czechoslovak context.

He said that the Marxist critique of power brought to light the hitherto unexplored connexions between political and economic power.

This discovery, together with the view of history as the history of class struggle, prepared the ground for social revolution, which has been expected to produce a new solution to the ancient problem of power. We have accomplished social revolution – and the problem of power continues. Though we have taken the 'bull by the horns' and we are holding him, somebody goes on kicking our backsides all the while.

Political power, 'a specifically human situation, affects the rulers and the ruled and threatens the health of both of them'. Experience of a thousand years has taught humanity certain 'traffic rules' of formal democracy. But the clearly drawn up blueprint of the mechanism of checks and balances may be distorted by the brutal power exercised by the owners of capital, or of guns, by family connexions, by monopoly of production. Distortion of the blueprint may result in the 'rude assertion that the rules of formal democracy are the cause of evil'. But those rules, according to Vaculík, are neither capitalist nor socialist. They are simply a humane invention, they are 'biased in favour of the ruled, but, when the government falls, they protect it against being shot'.

The government falls, and the citizen stands renewed. On the other hand, where the government stands for a long time, the citizen falls. Where does he fall? I will not try to please the enemy and say that he falls on the gallows. Only a few tens or hundreds of citizens do that. Our friends know that it is sufficient because it is followed by the fall of, perhaps, the whole nation, into fear, into political indifference and resignation, into petty daily cares and little desires, into dependence on gradually tinier and tinier overlords, into a serfdom of a new and unusual type, impossible to explain to a visitor from abroad. I think that there are no citizens in our country any longer. I have got proofs for that, collected over many years' work on newspapers and in broadcasting. I don't have to go far for a fresh reason. This congress did not take place when members of our organization decided, but when our master, after having considered the problems before him, gave us his kind permission. In return he expects, as has been the custom in the past thousands of years, that we shall pay tribute to his dynasty.

I suggest that everybody who will speak here always tells us how he imagines the thing that troubles him. Let us play the game of being citizens, now we have got the permission for it and this playground, and let us use the rest of our time as if we were of age and in the full possession of our legal rights.

I speak here as a citizen of a state I should never like to give up, but in which I cannot be content. I have in mind the affairs of the citizens, but here I am in a sensitive position. I am a member of the Communist Party as well, and I therefore should not and must not talk about party affairs. But it so happens that there is almost nothing that, at a certain point of the discussion, does not become a party affair. What can I do when both of them, my party and my government, have done their best to merge their agenda. It has also created a difficult situation for us, citizens assembled here. Party members are bound not to talk about important aspects of most key questions in front of non-members, who, in turn, have not got access to meetings when one can discuss those questions significantly, so that both sides are limited in their personal freedom to talk to each other as equals.

Vaculík then went on to say that

both our nations had been prepared by their whole history for socialism. And this state, after the end of the Second World War, was renewed as a political body that had only to organize itself on the basis of socialism. I will pass by the various dividing factors, but there was no other programme on the desk in 1945.

The rulers and the ruled should have been united.

The most interesting of the laws of political power, Vaculík said, a very definite law, described in literature thousands of times, is that

power prefers those people whose inner disposition is similar to its own. But because there is a lack of them, it must use other people as well, whom it adapts for its uses. Suitable for the purposes of power are, of course, people who desire power, further people obedient by nature, people with bad consciences, people whose desire for comfort, advantage and gain knows no moral conditions. It is possible to adapt frightened people with many children, people formerly degraded, who trustingly accept the offer of a new pride, further people who are naturally stupid. For a certain time, in certain circumstances and for certain purposes various moral absolutists and honest, but badly informed enthusiasts like myself may be temporarily used. The means for the adaptation of people are old, among them the sowing of general mistrust. Trust is divided into trust of first class, second class, third, and it is assumed that a mass of people exist who are not trusted at all. Information is also divided into quality groups: on pink paper, green paper, yellow paper, newspaper.

Power chose its people in Czechoslovakia. They were obedient people, people who made no difficulties, who asked no unexpected questions. Every selection produced the most average people. More complicated people, people with humour, charm, who could think for themselves, disappeared.

After criticizing the constitution of the country for its verbosity, obscurity and ineffectiveness, Vaculík said that,

Assuming that none of us was born for the sake of being governed easily, I suggest that the Union of Writers takes the initiative, possibly together with the Union of Journalists and other unions who work in similar fields, and ask the Czechoslovak Academy of Sciences for an expert opinion of the constitution, and demand, if necessary, its revision.

While I stand and talk here I have not got that free feeling that a person should have who says freely what he likes. I rather feel that, in a cowardly manner, I am exploiting some truce between the citizen and power, that I am sinning because some kind of closed season has been declared for writers and artists. How long it will last, I don't know: perhaps till the winter or till tomorrow. As I don't believe that citizens and political power can achieve identification, that the rulers and the ruled can meet for a sing-song, I don't believe that art and power will ever praise their having to live together. They cannot, will not, ever; they are different, not suited for each other.

But they may work out 'polite rules of intercourse'. 'Incompatibility does not necessarily mean enmity,' Vaculík added. Nevertheless, art

cannot give up its criticism of governments, because governments, the way they are, the manners they have, are the products of the civilization of peoples.

I see and hear how power retreats only where it sees and hears too strong a resistance. Not arguments, they will not convince it, but failure, repeated failure, when it wants to use the old ways of doing things. Failure, which always costs us money and nerves. I see constant good will and also constant danger that the bad old times will return.

On that day in the summer of 1967 Vaculík did not feel quite safe. He did not like the concept of 'autonomy for the arts' because of the thin line dividing the arts from politics. Some new and better laws have been passed, but the article on the draft law of freedom of assembly written for *Literární Noviny* had been censored.

I cannot see any guarantees. What kind of guarantees? I don't know. Here I will pause because I have got to the last thing, a great doubt. Do the ruling circles, the government itself and its members, have any guarantee of their personal freedoms, without which every creation is impossible, even the creation of policy? At this point my analysis of the laws of power becomes concluded, and I can only hint at a well known formula about the mill that sometimes grinds those who used to turn it.

The speeches of Kundera, Goldstücker, Liehm and Vaculík, Ivan Klíma's powerful denunciation of censorship, set the tone of the meetings. Hendrych's two speeches, at the beginning and on the last day of the congress, calling for deeper political engagement along the current party line, went unheeded. President Novotný ignored the writers' congress and instead he addressed the graduates of the party college in Prague on 30 June 1967, the day after the end of the writers' congress.

Though Novotný used the familiar formula about 'dogmatic influences at the early stage of socialist construction' he fiercely defended the past work of the party. He attacked the writers who had criticized the policy of the party and warned them that no deviations would be tolerated. Three days after Novotný had delivered his speech at the graduation ceremony, the trial of two writers and a student opened on 3 July. They were Pavel Tigrid, an American citizen of Czech origin, the editor of *Svědectví*, a magazine published in Paris, with wide circulation among Czechs and Slovaks living in the West; Jan Beneš, a thirty-one-year-old writer, who had been in custody since September 1966, and Karel Zámečník, a student at the film academy. On 15 July, the Prague municipal court sentenced Tigrid, *in absentia*, to fourteen years on charges of 'subversive activity and espionage'. Beneš, who had been accused of collaborating with Tigrid and of supplying him with information, received a sentence of five years, while Zámečník was acquitted.

President Novotný did not wait tor the outcome of the trial. He left, on 5 July, for a holiday in the Soviet Union.

4. The Slovaks and the Students

The existence of the writers on the one hand and of the Slovaks on the other was bad enough. Separately, they made a lot of trouble for President Novotný during his last months in power. But the thought that Slovak writers lived in his country must have appalled him.

Ladislav Mňačko was one of them. (Though born in Moravia, a few miles away from Ludvík Vaculík's birthplace, Mňačko has always written in Slovak.) The manuscript of his new novel, *A Taste of Power*, had been passed by the censor and set; the printers were then ordered to break up the block. The President had apparently taken the book too personally.

Since the publication of his outspoken, courageous short stories in 1964 Mňačko had acquired a high decoration – he became an 'artist of merit' in 1966 – as well as a flair for publicity. In the summer 1967 he went abroad, left the manuscript of his new novel with a publisher in Vienna, appeared on the local television, wrote an article criticizing Czechoslovak home and foreign policy, and on 10 August 1967 came to a temporary halt in Israel. On the following day he declared his intention of returning to Czechoslovakia as soon as she resumed diplomatic relations with Israel and of appearing, if necessary, before a court of law. On 16 August it was announced in Prague that Ladislav Mňačko had been deprived of Czechoslovak citizenship and expelled from the Communist Party. The title of 'artist of merit' was taken away from him, and his 'strong inclination to anarchy and serious moral defects' were mentioned in passing.

Later in the month President Novotný and his wife left on an official visit to Slovakia.

The Slovaks were celebrating an important historical occasion: the centenary of their high school and of the Matica, an organization that has been looking after Slovaks abroad. Novotný's speech at Turčanský Sv. Martin followed the usual pattern. He said that the nationality problem had been solved, adding statistics of Slovakia's economic growth to prove that Slovak interests were best served in a centralized Czechoslovak framework. He pointed out that Lenin himself regarded federation as a purely temporary measure. Turning his attention to foreign affairs, the President said that Czechoslovakia's policy in the Middle East was a part of anti-imperialist struggle, and not an antisemitic drive. He drew a bold historical parallel between the role of western powers at the time of Munich and again in 1967: they had supported aggressive Hitler in 1938 and they were again supporting Israel's aggression now.

Novotný touched on the two most sensitive subjects in a way that pleased few people in the audience. After his speech he talked to Vasil Bilak, a secretary to the Slovak Communist Party, about Matica. Bilak complained that the old Matica building was too small; Novotný suggested that its papers should be transferred to Prague, and that, anyway, the Foreign Institute (*Zahraniční Ústav*) should look after the Czechs and Slovaks living abroad. This suggestion made Bilak angry, and he asked Novotný, rather loudly, how dare he make such an offensive suggestion. The President and his wife left the celebration early, as soon as their car and driver were found.

Novotný's behaviour, the tone of his speech, were totally unsuitable for a Slovak national celebration. The knowledge that the Czechs and the Slovaks are two separate peoples has been slow in coming to Prague. Until 1918 the two nations had had little in common. The Slovaks lived in the Hungarian part of the Habsburg monarchy; the Czechs in the Austrian.

Whereas the Czechs had had historical memories of their own state, the Slovaks had none. For centuries the Slovaks had led the lives of a subject peasant population, divided among their lords, the Hungarian landowners. Some of the biggest of the landed properties of the Magyar magnates were in Slovakia; Kossuth was a Slovak-born Hungarian. From the middle of the nineteenth century, the Slovaks went through a national revival similar to that of the Czechs. They produced their first poets, their first historians. The Protestant minority played an important role in the revival.

The rapid industrialization that gave the Czech national consciousness its dynamic quality was absent in Slovakia. Links were forged between Czech and Slovak writers and intellectuals. The Czechs were fascinated by the similarity of their two languages and they admired Slovak folklore, especially the fairy tales, improved upon during many long winter evenings. The Slovaks remembered no princes and kings of their own; the heroes of their historical memories were the primitive peasant rebels, the symbols and catalysts of national and social rebellion. Jánošík, the most famous of them all, symbolized the fierce personal independence of the Slovaks. Sentenced to the slowest death by hanging, he was pardoned when half dead. He told the executioner who came to take him off the hook to go away and leave him to die in peace.

Invasions by the Turks, peasant rebellions, Catholic religion, Hungarian landlords, large-scale emigration to America, and above all, ceaseless labour in the fields and the woods, have all marked deeply the life and character of the Slovak people. They can be harder and more direct than the Czechs; they have little calculating carefulness in them, and they do not suffer from second thoughts.

During the First World War the societies of Slovak immigrants in the United States were won over to the cause of a united Czech and Slovak independent state. Thomas Masaryk, the former professor of philosophy at Prague university and deputy to the parliament in Vienna, did a lot of the persuading. Masaryk's credentials were good; his father was Slovak, his wife American. On 31 May 1918 representatives of the organizations of Czech and Slovak immigrants met Masaryk in Pittsburg to talk to him about the shape of the future Czechoslovak state. The Slovaks wanted some assurance that the numerically much stronger Czechs would not try to assimilate them. Masaryk drafted the nationality policy of the future state straightaway. Slovakia was to have her own administration, judicial system and language; the details of the arrangement would be worked out by the representatives of the two peoples in the liberated republic. (All this was happening several months before the creation of the Czechoslovak state at the end of the First World War.)

One of the Slovaks then asked for a 'Diet', and the demand was inserted by Masaryk into his draft of the controversial Pittsburg Convention. Masaryk signed it on 14 November 1918, the day of his election as President, and shortly before his departure from the United States. Together with Masaryk and Beneš, Milan Štefánik, a Slovak astronomer who had been working in France before the First World War, contributed to the cause of Czechoslovak independence. This gentle astronomer, who became interested in military matters and flying and reached the rank of a French general, flew back to his newly liberated country and crashed shortly after having crossed its frontier.

The rumour that the crash had been engineered by the new government in Prague established itself as a part of the undergrowth of central European myths between the two world wars. It bears witness to the bitterness that arose between the Czechs and the Slovaks during the first years of their life together in a common state. The parliament in Prague worked out a centralist constitution, and the government put it into an even more centralizing practice. The autonomist party in Slovakia, led by a Catholic priest, Andrew Hlinka, used the

Pittsburg Convention to remind the government in Prague of Masaryk's original intentions. It annoyed the ageing President so much that in a letter to Hlinka he described the Convention as a 'forgery'.

The 'nationality policy' of the Czechoslovak Republic in the twenty years between the two wars was meant mainly for the Germans, and then the Hungarians: never for the Slovaks. It was assumed that a 'Czechoslovak' nationality would emerge, sooner or later, and the whole problem could stay shelved. Hitler's satellite state of Slovakia during the Second World War was built on the resentment of the Slovaks against the Czechs, and in that way, the idea of an autonomous Slovakia acquired a bad odour.

But while the autonomous 'populist' party had sold out to the Nazis, thousands of Slovaks fought Hitler's Germany in their own country. With the exception of eastern Moravia in the later stages of the war, Czech resistance was largely confined to the gathering of intelligence and keeping the communications with the exile government in London open, sabotage in factories and sporadic attacks on Nazi officials. In Slovakia, with its mountains and impenetrable forests, a partisan movement started to develop towards the end of 1942. A year later the Slovak national council was formed, with three communists and three middle-class representatives on it. In March 1944 the Czechoslovak ambassador to Moscow began to negotiate with the Russians about the supply of arms in the event of a Slovak uprising; in August a delegation of the national council boarded a plane on an airfield in Slovakia and flew to Moscow. By that time, large territory in the central and eastern districts was controlled by the partisans. On 29 August 1944 German units started to cross the frontiers; by the end of October they had occupied a large part of Slovakia, and the national council ordered a return to the partisan mode of fighting. The Slovak rebels withdrew into the mountains and awaited the arrival of the Red Army.

The experiment in autonomy, under Hitler's protection, ended early in 1945, but not so the desire of the Slovaks to be respected and regarded as a separate nation. The Czechs in the new government did not take it seriously. Edward Beneš, Masaryk's friend and successor, was unable to pass beyond the official attitude to the Slovak question in the first Republic. Towards the end of the Second World War, as the Red Army was approaching Slovak territory, Beneš moved his government from London to Moscow, where it worked out its first programme. In March 1945 members of the Slovak national council suggested the transformation of Czechoslovakia into a federal state. The Slovak national council was to go on existing, and it was to have its own executive organ, the council of commissioners. The Czechs were to have similar institutions and above the two there was to be a common parliament and government, which would deal with foreign trade, defence and communications, all the common questions concerning Bohemia, Moravia and Slovakia.

But Beneš and the Czech politicians would have nothing of that. They dismissed the Slovak suggestion as leading direct to 'dualism' or 'federalism'. They were right. It would have done. In 1947 the Slovaks had to remind Beneš, then the President, that the 'lives of the Czechs and the Slovaks together in a common state cannot be dictated by the demands and the needs of the Czechs alone'.

Of the big political parties before the war, the communists found it easier than anyone else to accept the existence of the two peoples. But they, too, were divided. At the time of the negotiations in Moscow in the spring of 1945 Gustav Husák, a Slovak communist, was the most forceful advocate of federalism, but his ideas found little response among his Czech comrades.

In that way, a curious lopsided practice developed in post-war Czechoslovakia, which still survives in the organization of the Communist Party. After the war the Slovaks got their committee of plenipotentiaries, a local duplicate of the government in Prague, but the Czechs did not set up similar local organs. They had the central Czechoslovak government in Prague instead. In the same way, there are now the Slovak Communist Party and the Czechoslovak Party. But there existed no Czech Communist Party for Bohemia and Moravia alone. The administrative lopsidedness showed that the Czechs had not given up their dream of a united, Czech and Slovak, nation.

It may be that such an aim was neither desirable nor practicable at the best of times. The events of the past twenty years have ruled it out. The first intimations of trouble came through in 1950. In that year three leading Slovak communists, Gustav Husák, Laco Novomeský and Vlado Clementis, were accused of 'bourgeois nationalism', of wanting to destroy the unity of the Czechoslovak Republic. It was a serious and quite absurd charge. Less than two years later Clementis, who had succeeded Jan Masaryk as the Minister of Foreign Affairs, was sentenced to death. In 1954, during a new wave of arrests and show trials of Slovak communists, Antonín Novotný accused them of having 'come to an agreement with the descendants of the Habsburgs and other unworthy elements in the services of the imperialist war-mongers'. In 1952 the trials had been arranged under the supervision of Stalin's and Beria's men; two years later, the Czechs were running the trials on their own. The official line in the Novotný era was that the nationality problem had been successfully solved; the charge of 'bourgeois nationalism' was used as occasion arose. It was trundled out, for the last time, by President Novotný in the autumn of 1967. The nationality of the leading officials in the party and the state had been surrounded by a kind of official coyness; people in high positions were presented as national hermaphrodites, a condition that sometimes affected even their accents, a mid-Moravian approximation of the two languages. A young Czech historian has recently written of the old nationality policy that 'everyone behaves as if the Slovaks were still a separate people, but just about to merge into some common nationality'. (Milan Hübl in *Literární Listy*, 14 March 1968.)

When Alexander Dubček succeeded Novotný as the first secretary of the Communist Party in January 1968 he was the first Slovak to occupy a key position in the party and with that, in the state. The Prime Minister at the time, Lenárt, also happened to be a Slovak. Apart from the Minister of Building, however, no Slovak was in charge of an important Ministry in the Prague government. This did not stop the chauvinist Czechs from making disturbed noises ('The Slovaks are ruling us now!') while like-minded Slovaks derived quiet pleasure from the situation. It did not last long. There was no place for Lenárt in the new government announced in April 1968. Towards the end of the summer of 1967, Novotný and his friends could no longer regain the confidence of the Slovaks. It was a question of time before an opponent of Novotný would emerge in the central committee of the Communist Party. The right man was certain of solid support by the Slovaks.

Novotný's actions at that time had a certain compulsive, relentless quality about them. After the fiasco of his Slovak visit he addressed the problem of the recalcitrant writers. He used for that purpose the unfortunate Jiří Hendrych, who had failed to impose order on the party intellectuals at the congress in June. He had made a fool of himself there, in the course of a few emotional outbursts. On 26 and 27 September Hendrych convened the central committee to approve punitive measures against the writers and their Union.

The party made an attempt to cut down the manifold activities of the Czechoslovak Writers' Union. The Ministry of Culture took over its successful weekly *Literární Noviny*, and started publishing it under a different name and a new editorial board. The allocation of paper to the Union's publishing house was to be cut down by 300 tons. After hard bargaining a cut of 140 tons only was agreed on. The setting up of two new houses and personal reshuffles in the Prague publishing world, aimed at weakening the position of the Union's own firm. The literary fund, meant for writers who needed it, was to be taken over by the Ministry as well. Ludvík Vaculík, Antonín Liehm and Ivan Klíma were expelled from the party.

The Union however fought hard to defend itself. Apart from expulsion from the party and annoying restrictions – Liehm for instance was refused a passport for a visit to West Germany – no further measures were taken against the writers. The old scheme of power, the whole system of one party under one leader with one policy was not what it used to be. No doubt comparative prosperity helped. Ivan Sviták, for instance, who had lost his job in the philosophical institute of the Czechoslovak Academy of Sciences for his political views, simply sold his car and went to ground, in meagre comfort, as a kind of *Privatgelehrter* of old. Nor did the writers' expulsion from the party mean that they were absolutely cut off from society and sources of income. They remained free and went on writing, with their Union and its funds behind them, waiting for the weather to clear.

Soon the incompetence of the government, its frozen inflexibility, was revealed in a different context. This time the quality of Novotný's state was tested by the kind of lives young people lived in it.

In the first years of the present decade, young people differed from the rest of Czech society only by their age. They were not yet a sharply defined, isolated group; there were as yet no signs of a world-wide rebellion. The official organization, the Union of Czechoslovak Youth, was moribund. Its membership in 1960, 57 per cent of all the young people in the age groups catered for by the Union, had declined by 1967 to 26 per cent. Many of its officials were people without higher education, in steady jobs, with one foot in middle age. The chairman of the Union, still in office in March 1968, was thirty-six years old and had first gone to work there eighteen years ago. The interest the party leaders took in the youth movement was often trivial: on one occasion a former first secretary to the central committee said about a candidate for the leadership of the Union that he 'wasn't handsome enough', and therefore should not have the job. A few years ago, the movement's organizers received a directive from the centre to organize 'auxiliary police units'. The original intention was that they would look after young offenders but as the units grew they were used for more questionable purposes. They were encouraged to spy on other young people, took part in demonstrations, cooperated with the police during various searches, gave evidence in courts. The work of these units more and more came to resemble the work of the police, and some of their members eventually became policemen. Young people knew of the existence of the auxiliary units and they naturally resented it. It was for them further evidence of the way their elders, people in authority, wanted to use youth for their own frivolous purposes.

In the Petřín park, the wooded hill to the south of the castle, there is a statue of a young man, his head inclined, smelling lilac. It is Karel Hynek Mácha, the author of the very popular romantic poem called *May*, who died young. The youth of Prague paid annual homage to him on the first day in May. They usually ran into trouble with the police, more serious in 1966 than any other year. On 1 May 1966 students, apprentices, clerks, workers, most of them between 17 and 23 years old, marched from Petřín across the bridge into the centre of the town. Shouts like, 'We want freedom, we want democracy', 'A good communist is a dead communist', were overheard; policemen were called 'Gestapo', and a small red flag decorating a tram was burnt. The crowd of a few hundred young men and girls marched to Václavské náměstí, stopped a few trams on the way, and came to a halt at the equestrian statue of St Wenceslas at the far end of the square. There were members of the 'auxiliary units' of the youth movement among the crowd and advice to watch out was passed on.

On 24 May 1966 the municipal court in Prague tried a group of twelve young people. They were all found guilty and received sentences from 5 to 17 months, on evidence largely from members of the 'auxiliary units'. One of the girls later talked about the frightfulness of her life after the sentence. She arrived at the first prison during a rebellion by the inmates, who had been given mouldy soup for lunch; she shared her cell with a young prostitute, who usually addressed her as 'you whore'. Then she was transferred to a 'corrective camp' – a Borstal-type institution which seems to have contained older women as well – where she spent her days threading beads and her nights fending off the passes by the many resident lesbians.

I keep on thinking that I could not survive it for a second time, I don't trust people since then. Indifferent is what I became there, got used to rude words, somehow I am afraid of love. They discharged me conditionally, but I didn't sign anything to say that I wouldn't talk about it later. I even refused to sign the medical certificate, because you don't know what you may catch at a place like that. I caught impetigo. [*Literární Listy*, 25 March 1968].

There was a certain suspicious neatness about the trials of young people in those years. The police and the courts were controlled by the same authority, and it was enough for an official at the Ministry of Interior 'to lift the telephone receiver and give an order'. On a lower level members of the 'auxiliary units' both took part in the demonstrations (who knows what they shouted themselves) and gave evidence to the court.

In 1963 students from the departments of philosophy, natural sciences, law, mechanical engineering and nuclear physics at Prague university formed the 'five departments group', which did much to reintroduce politics into students' life. At a conference of university students in 1966 Jiří Müller, of the department of mechanical engineering, said that the policy of the youth organization must 'not confine itself to declarations in favour of socialism and with that, of the aims of the party. It must put across real views of young people on the *ways* the party choose for the realization of those aims. If need be, the Union must oppose the policy of the party' *(Literární Listy*, 7 March 1968.) Müller's suggestions as to the reform of the youth organization included federalization according to age and occupation groups; his demand that the Union should have a policy of its own came up again and again in his speech. Müller's views were shared by Oskar Novotný, a law student from Bratislava, and many others.

In the meantime, the 1966 May Day demonstrations and the subsequent trials took place. At the end of the year, Müller was sent down by his university, expelled from the youth organization and called up to do his national service. Six months later, Luboš Holeček, Müller's colleague and closest friend, received the same treatment. In the spring of 1968, the two boys were still wearing their army uniforms. The measures taken against them transformed uncoordinated expressions of resentment into a movement. The Union had been planning a congress, and the preliminary meetings often became stormy demonstrations against the way Müller's case had been handled by the authorities. The students kept on attacking the official leadership of the youth organization.

Its fifth congress opened in Prague on 5 June 1967, a few weeks before the writers' conference. The Soviet delegation was led by Marshal Koniev; President Novotný addressed the five thousand delegates and guests. There were to be no experiments with federation, the Union was to remain united and under the direct control of the party. Before the opening of the congress the party had issued instructions to the Union's officials. Müller was said to have conducted the policy of a 'pro-China faction'; the officials were asked to keep the students in their places. The writers were wrong if they believed that the summer of 1967 was a closed season for the intellectuals. On the contrary.

When one of the youth movement officials was asked why Müller was expelled he replied frankly that 'Comrade Müller, like every other member of the Union, had the right openly to express his opinions. It should be said, however, that at the time when he did so, such behaviour was not common in political work.'

Jiří Müller however did not accept his condemnation without a fight. He appealed to the party, and received the following reply from Martin Vaculík (no relation to Ludvík Vaculík, the writer), the leading secretary of the district party commitee in Prague:

I have received your letter in which you appeal against the expulsion from the university and the youth organization, to the district committee of the Communist Party. It is my view that the university and youth movement organs are fully competent in regard to the matter. You have remembered the existence of the party district committee rather late. You should have turned to us when you were preparing and thinking about the actions that came into conflict with the interests of the party, the students and the youth movement. That was the right time for talks and consultations. Now you are reaping the fruit of your activity. The party condemns no one, and does not condemn you. Insofar as you speak of the rights of the citizen, we have always understood them as indivisible from his duties. Your appeal absolutely lacks this consciousness of civic duty, as well as any hint of self-criticism. With comradely greetings
Martin Vaculík.

Young people found it hard to understand the moral turpitude of their elders. They felt that something incredible, discreditable, was going on in the world of authority. Many men had been deceived or frightened into connivance with Hitler, genocide, senseless wars, the most blatant abuses of justice. Many had faith in the ultimate goal and let the means look after themselves. Young people in Czechoslovakia care little for the symmetry of the old abstractions. With a sharp sense of reality, of individual beings, they have brought the means back under close surveillance. Their economic independence – students in Czechoslovakia have some of it and they will want more – adds to their need for freedom. Heavy-handed paternalism is out of place when the father does not have to tighten his belt or dip into the family fortune to provide for the education, for any kind of future, of his children. Martin Vaculík, who made an unwise attempt to replace the fathers of many, became the laughing-stock of young people in Prague.

The ground had been prepared for a severe clash between the students and the state. It took place on 31 October 1967. A short walk from the castle, beyond the Strahov monastery and the Habsburg-built barracks, there are the biggest students' residences in Prague. A bleak, uninviting but serviceable place. The electricity supply was liable to be cut off from time to time, and when it happened in the evenings, the students either got cross and shouted, or went out for a drink. On Tuesday 31 October, there was a meeting of the students' council with journalists, who came to see the conditions in the residences for themselves. The light stayed on till about 9 p.m., then went out. There were the usual shouts, whistling, a few bits of paper on fire floated down from the windows. Groups of people started gathering outside, shouts of 'Let's all go out!' were heard. A procession formed, walked round the buildings, shouting, 'Let's go out, we want light!'

Carrying candles, playing various musical instruments, the students began marching towards town. Before they reached the steep Nerudova street, when they had to choose between going down the street or walking on towards the castle, counsels of prudence prevailed. The procession started moving towards Nerudova. Before they reached its end, the police squads began to arrive.

The students tried to explain to the police why they were

demonstrating. The policemen told them to choose a few representatives, who would be taken to the appropriate place where they could complain. The announcement was greeted by a roar of laughter. Said one of the students later,

One would have had to be really naïve to swallow that. It was obvious what would have happened. Those people would have been at once accused of having organized the whole thing, they would perhaps have been sent down, or I don't know what would have happened to them. The same as happened to those who had been accused of having organized the May demonstrations and other actions. So that nobody could really trust that suggestion ... [*Student*, 3 April 1968].

The students did not move after the police had made their offer. They stood around, facing the police, shouting a bit, the street was full of them. Then they began turning round and started the long climb back. As they were walking up Nerudova, police cars kept on driving up and down, forcing the students to keep to the pavements. One of the complaints of the police later was that the students were blocking the flow of traffic. The policemen kept on dispersing groups of young people, and arrested three of them. The arrests sparked off the trouble. The policemen started making remarks, 'We know what kind of bloody light you want', and 'It's a political demonstration', and 'The students are wanting something again'. A representative of the students' council went to negotiate the release of the arrested men; two of them were allowed to go. No officer was present at the time, only lower ranks. Controversies kept on breaking out, the students swore at the police, the policemen chased the students. Somebody shouted, 'They've still got one of us', the students started again marching down the road, shouting. The policemen tried to break the procession up; there were too few of them there, and they failed. They got into their cars, made a road block further down the road. Vile abuse was shouted freely from both sides. Police reinforcements arrived on the scene and tried pushing the students back to their residences. The students started running back, then some of them sat down just on the other side of the entrance gate. They thought they were safe there, on academic ground.

The police began beating the students as soon as they reached them. They thrashed about with their truncheons. Fights broke out inside and outside the buildings. The policemen tended to keep away from bigger groups of young people, but chased and beat up individuals. They used their tear gas sprays against the students, and beat up men and women indiscriminately.

In the small hours of Wednesday morning, the noises of pursuit and battle at last died down. Twelve students and three policemen were taken to a hospital. Prague dailies reported the incident on 2 and 3 November; the official report was published on 15 December 1967. The press secretary to the government remarked that 'we must oppose attempts to exploit those events against the interests of socialist society'. (*Reportér*, 6–13 March 1968.)

At the Petřín hospital, where the injured had been taken, the doctors discussed the incident at their meeting on the morning of 1 November. The chief surgeon expressed the view that the police had gone too far. Two of the injured students had severe concussion, one of them was unconscious on arrival. One medical report stated that the injured had received 'lacerations on the left hand and left shoulder after an attack upon him by an unidentified uniformed person'.

A short time after the demonstration on 31 October rumours started to circulate in Prague that the students were arming themselves, and that the Strahov incident had been inspired, and perhaps paid for, by foreign enemies. The students were warned that the workers would put them in their places, and that the workers' militia would move into action. Such rumours and threats apparently originated from the highest level of the party. By way of an explanation, it was said that there was a government reception at the castle on the night of the Strahov incident, and the policemen were anxious to keep the students away from there.

On 9 November 1967 students at the philosophical faculty held a five hours' meeting, when they discussed the Strahov incident. They sent a letter to the Minister of Education, asking that the policemen responsible for the beatings should be identified and punished, that they should not be allowed to use tear gas or any other chemical weapons, and that they should wear number-tags for easy identification.

Soon after I arrived in Prague on 2 April 1968 policemen started wearing on their coats shining new metal discs, with their numbers.

5. A Programmed Revolution

The Czechs themselves do not like using the word 'revolution' for the recent events in their country. Neither a spontaneous outbreak of popular unrest, nor a palace revolution, nor any of their combinations, have taken place in Czechoslovakia.

Views had been exchanged before banners appeared in the streets. The unrest began among the usually peaceful, law-abiding people. In newspaper offices; at writers' desks; in television studios; in laboratories, in lecture rooms; in economists' calculations. It began as a 'revolution of the intellectuals', but the intellectuals were neither called upon to man barricades nor take over full responsibility for the government of the country.

Very near the Union of Czechoslovak Writers, a grim nineteenth-century building houses the Academy of Sciences. Founded in 1952, with a large budget and the right to grant degrees, the Academy has distinguished ancestors in the Royal Learned Society and the Czech Academy of Arts and Sciences. Not all their members were coopted by the Academy. At the time of its foundation, the conflict between the learned men inside and outside the party was sharp, and political criteria were used for the selection of members. Scholars with international reputations were passed over: academicians were elected who had one or two articles or political pamphlets to their credit. The conflict between the communists and the non-communists was sharper in the arts than in the sciences, especially in those disciplines, such as law, with points of contact with politics.

But the differences and vendettas of the early years of the

Academy's existence are of little interest to the younger scientists and scholars. The middle generation have been taught by the men who may have suffered academic injustice in the past. But they have problems and controversies of their own. They disliked, for instance, the way Novotný interfered with the business of the Academy in 1960. They do not mind helping the politicians with concrete problems of physical and social sciences, but prefer traffic in advice going one way.

Some of them have quarrelled with the writers. Living next to each other, the writers knew what the learned men were doing, and the scholars watched closely the writers' activities. In the Academy, the moderate reform group was well represented; the writers tended to be more radical. Both groups had direct links with the party leadership, usually passing through the ideological section, the most sensitive department of the party in the last years of President Novotný's rule. Its heads kept on falling, one after the other. They were under a continuous double pressure. The party leaders wanted conformity among the intellectuals, who, in their turn, wanted freedom of inquiry and expression. Both the intellectuals and the party expected the head of the ideological section to please them. Many people, a few of them distinguished and intelligent, found out that it was difficult to do so.

An historian by training, Pavel Auersperg had been Novotný's private secretary and speech writer until January 1965, when he was appointed the head of the ideological section. He held the job down until March 1967. Though his allegiance was to the party and its line in the first place, Auersperg was an intellectual, and came more and more under the influence of his friends. Towards the end of his term in office, Auersperg is reported to have met the Russian historian and diplomat Udaltsov and the press attaché. They talked about liberalization in Czechoslovakia and about the anti-Soviet tendencies of Czech communist journalists. The conversation ended in a late-night quarrel at one of the Prague wine cellars.

Nevertheless, a few months later, after he had lost his job in the ideological section, he remarked bitterly to a meeting, 'Comrades, what I can no longer bear hearing, is the word reform!' The pressures on Auersperg were strong, and he found the pace hard to take. As a communist of middle-class origin, he may have been under additional strain.

Nevertheless, when Auersperg was in office one or two important projects were launched in the social sciences. Towards the end of 1966 the Academy set up a research team to inquire into changes in the Czechoslovak political system that should follow economic reforms. Its findings are to be ready at the end of 1968. The team has been conducting polls to find out about people's attitudes to the electoral system, political institutions, etc. On 28 July 1967, when its members discussed their work on Radio Prague, one of them remarked that the simplest opinion poll would establish that people regarded their political system as unsatisfactory.

The head of the team Zdeněk Mlynář, lawyer and politologue at the Academy, had on a few occasions crossed swords with the writers. Mlynář had been in close touch with Auersperg, whom he had helped in the attempt to make the old *Literární Noviny* toe the party line early in 1966, and the writers have not forgiven him for that. Nevertheless, when Mlynář was asked by the ideological section to give an expert opinion on the speech by Vaculík at the writers' congress, he refused to do so.

With their comprehensive view of the difficulties facing reform in Czechoslovakia, Mlynář and his friends have often taken the path of a tactical compromise. It sometimes led them to support conservative policies, in undesirable company. Mlynář has made a public apology. A member of the staff of *Literární Noviny* accused Auersperg and Mlynář of regarding the editors of the writers' weekly as

mad chaps, who mess around with politics without knowing the rules, thus helping the dogmatists in the party and jeopardizing the work of the progressive communists. In line with Auersperg's policy, now collapsed, we were forbidden to criticize in our newspaper the draft of the press law, to oppose the internal directive, which, illegally, made that miserable law still sharper, to criticize twenty years of electoral farce, etc., all things that have been now discarded even by Auersperg and Mlynář. Mlynář of course then knew what we were doing, in fact knew much more, because he, and Auersperg especially, used to tell us that we don't know everything. And that was the mean thing, that we were never allowed to know everything. Mlynář is cleverer than I am, I shall give him that, because he is on the [Academy] team and I am not. What he is after nowadays, as far as I understand it, I shall support for the time being, but I shall not enter into any obligations. I also know that one must compromise in politics, but making compromise one's aim is contemptible. I know that tactics exist and that men who make them honourably are useful because they help to overcome points of crisis or inactivity. But I think that people without tactics are absolutely essential in a normal situation. Because otherwise nobody would know who in the nation wants what and how much, and the politicians could pack up and go home. [Vaculík's letter in *Literární Listy*, 21 March 1968]

Mlynář and his team have not yet finished their work that will doubtless be based on the views of the 'people without tactics'. But before Mlynář got down to work on his project Radovan Richta of the philosophical institute at the Academy of Sciences, and his team, had completed their commission in 1966. The large group (twenty-five men and three women) contained economists, sociologists, an historian, an architect, a physicist, a cybernetics expert, a statistician and other scholars. It concerned itself with the scientific and technical revolutions and their impact on society, and it published its findings under the title *Civilization at the Crossroads*. The introduction briefly surveyed the work being done in the West and pointed out that socialist countries had for some time tended to neglect the problems of post-industrial society. Nevertheless, the authors had at hand the classical quotation by the President of the Soviet Academy of Sciences, on the scale of priorities in a modern state.

In the new historical situation ... it is necessary that technology should grow and develop faster than heavy industry, and that material sciences, which form the principal basis of all technical progress, being the main source of the most important technological ideas, should grow at a faster rate than technology. [*Pravda*, 13 June 1961]

Richta's inquiry was aware of the dangers of transposing precise scientific terms into the looser context of social sciences. This method avoided many of those dangers, and the team stated their case in a forceful manner.

The study, *Civilization at the Crossroads*, argued that the old, traditional situation of industrial society, the double line-up of man and machines, is becoming a thing of the past. Czechoslovakia is now at the threshold of the scientific-technological revolution, but the authors issued a stern warning that the development is far from automatic. It could be impeded, or deflected altogether. Czechoslovak industrial management, because of its low quality, had been unable to understand the nature of the transition. It would try to 'push society back into the ways of extensive industrialization'.

In Czechoslovakia over the past years the 'development of the forces of production was directed, in a one-sided way, to the increase of the number of industrial objects with the traditional structure of production forces – too demanding of investment, labour, sources of raw materials, etc.' The means of acceleration (the employment of sciences, the development of human capacities, etc.) have been left largely unexploited. Industrial development tied down too much labour, and the growth of production was unsatisfactory. The study group argued that by 1958 or 1959 at the latest the opportunities for an extensive industrial development had been exhausted in Czechoslovakia. The old 'administrative-

directive system of management' found the point of transformation of an industrial into a scientific-technological
system beyond its scope.

Czechoslovakia, in comparison with other countries, now
operates a relatively small amount of automated equipment.
About seventy per cent of her machine industry, for instance, is
based on individual piece or short-run production, and going
over to automation would require a complex bridging process. As it is, the Academy of Sciences study group
estimated that the automation of machine industry in Czechoslovakia is 3 to 6 times less developed than in America; the
production of automation systems by the electronic industry
is 2 to 3 times lower than in advanced countries; in the
highest forms of automation, cybernetics, production in
Czechoslovakia is fifty times lower than in the U.S.A. and 10
to 15 times lower than in England, France or Sweden. The
Czechs produce 3 to 4 times less plastic materials than America
or West Germany, and their textile industry uses 4 times less
man-made fibres than Japan or France.

While the socialist countries faced the necessity of industrialization, developed capitalist countries had the choice before
them of either using the opportunities offered to them by the
technological revolution, or stagnating. The gap between the
two systems seems to be lengthening; Khrushchev's optimistic
pronouncements are things of the past. The Czech scientists
calculated the level of productivity of labour in socialist
countries as being 2 to 3 times lower than in America, and
that if the rate of growth were maintained, the overtaking of
the capitalist system would take 'about 20 or 30 years, or
more'. In the competition of the two systems, the technological revolution will turn against anyone who cannot
keep up the pace.

It was implied in the study that dogmatism was out, and
elastic, empirical attitudes were in. The Czechs know that it is
essential to create a social fabric so sensitive, a society so

flexible, that it would easily respond to the requirements of change. Under a certain level, the members of the study group argue, concentration of all the means in industry – the expansion of the industrial society's double line-up, of the production line and of the supply of men serving it – is best for growth. Above a certain level, exactly the opposite is true. The means released from production, rather than the means put into it, is what matters. Skills, qualifications, the determination to have them and use them, are now at a premium. According to a Soviet calculation, an average scientist equals 36 workers in a year. 'The traditional employment of man as an unskilled labour unit therefore necessarily becomes, in one section after another, a brake on the forces of production and an uneconomic waste of human abilities.' As automation excludes man from the process of production, the whole structure of society begins to change.

The old, one-shot improvements of the means of production since, say, the invention of the wheel, followed by a rest on past achievements, the whole system of jerky advancement, is now replaced by a continuous and universal change. The permanent revolution will not take place in politics, but in science. Such are the implications of the study: so far, the politicians have used the scientists; from now on, science will make the pace for politics. One of the main tasks of the party will be to open up and keep clear the paths for the advancement of science.

The economic views expressed in *Civilization at the Cross-roads* reflected the current thinking in Czechoslovakia. When Richta's group was working on its study, the construction of the New Economic Model was in its last stages. The economists at the Academy of Sciences, under Professor Oto Šik, had led their colleagues in their attempts to reform the old system. Economic disaster, and Novotný's belief that it could be dealt with in isolation, opened up a gap in the door.

Professor Šik, a diminutive person with a strong sense of purpose, now forty-nine years old, was born in Pilsen. He was interested in economics as a schoolboy, and the subject still fascinates him. Like Novotný and Hendrych, Šik spent the best part of the war at Mauthausen; after the war he taught political economy at several universities, becoming in 1960 a corresponding member of the Academy of Sciences. Two years later he became a member of the central committee of the Communist Party and the director of the Economic Institute of the Academy. In March 1964 he was transferred from the ideological to the economic section of the central committee and in the same year published his second important study, *Problems of Commodity Relations in a Socialist Economy*. Professor Šik was in mild trouble in the early 1950s. In a broadcast interview he said recently that 'there were months, even years when I was not allowed to enter party organizations, when I was not delegated, though it was never publicly declared. . . .' Ten years later, he became the principal source of new economic ideas in the country.

The old economic system in Czechoslovakia created its own prefabricated market; the forces of the market place were suspended. Rigid long-term central planning of an extensive economy was underpinned by the assignation of targets and the allocation of commodities needed for production. Factories were cartelized in 'associations', under 'industrial boards of directors'. The boards were equipped with comprehensive powers. They could impose levies on the revenues of the individual factories under their control, and in that way they were able to channel revenue from more to less profitable firms. In such a system prices made sense only to those people who were responsible for fixing them. In addition Czechoslovakia became a workshop for processing Soviet raw materials. Trade agreements with Russia were built into domestic planning. (cf. Vaclav Holesovsky's excellent article

'Planning Reforms in Czechoslovakia' in *Soviet Studies*, April 1968.)

Whatever the flaws of the system may have been, an army of bureaucrats became accustomed to operating it and many men came to have a vested interest in its preservation. The 'cadre policy' of the party prized the possession of the right kind of political views above technical qualifications; the practice, after 1948, of rewarding political services by jobs in the nationalized enterprises was not as sound as it had seemed at first. According to the well publicized admissions by Novotný's government, decline in quality as well as a growing technological lag was the outcome of the old system. The Russians started shopping around elsewhere for finished articles, while the Czechs remained dependent on Russian raw materials.

The discussion of Czechoslovakia's economy which opened in the autumn of 1963 came several years too late. When it did come, it was an open but rather one-sided debate. The reformers talked while the practitioners of the old system kept silent. In September 1964 'draft principles' for improvement were published, and they were accepted by the central committee on 30 January 1965. Throughout that year economists were working out the details of their proposals. The measures were to remain operative from 1966 till the end of 1968. In addition – and that was their major victory, in the summer of 1966 – the reformers made the party leadership agree to a readjustment of prices, without which, they felt, the success or failure of their work would be hard to assess. The second set of reforms followed, and were passed as enabling acts, to remain in force in the years 1967 to 1970. By the end of 1966 the New Economic Model was complete. It only remained to test it in practice.

One of the main criticisms of the old system was that it resulted in pseudo-planning. It pushed the economy in a certain direction, and that was all. The thinking behind it was cluttered up with considerations that had nothing to do with the economy.

Since 1957, the Soviet economic practice of 'conspicuous production', the whole system of command planning, has been examined in detail by a number of western economists, and found defective. (The phrase is Professor Michael Polanyi's. cf. *Survey*, October–December 1960.) The Czech economists, like many of their colleagues in other European countries, have been thinking on the same lines. Their pronouncements are full of gallicisms and anglicisms. They are more than half-way back to Professor Hayek's belief that the market is the cheapest planner and controller, but not all the way. The Czech reformers believe that good planning means the attainment of objectives, and they have put the satisfaction of the consumer in the top place on their list of priorities. They maintain that, in the conditions created by their new model, planning will come into its own. They do not see their planners becoming mere chroniclers of the happenings in the market place. They are thinking in terms of a 'sliding plan' covering several years but corrected as need be according to past experience. But their immediate problem has been, and still is, to give the country a 'socialist market economy' in good working order.

It is not only a question of dismantling the old system of material allocation, but mainly of creating a market in which buyers and sellers will find each other. The powers of the boards of directors of the various 'associations' have to be curtailed, and the autonomy of the various factories has to be restored. This requires an almost inhuman self-discipline on the part of the directors. They are expected to give up many of their powers, to break up, in effect, their empires, and then wean the factories away from the old system. Under the New Economic Model the factories have to do more than produce. They have to deal with their suppliers and customers direct. They may well be fearful of their new freedom. They would use it, the reformers feared, to raise their prices. Prices were therefore to stay under strict control, which immediately raised a new problem, of how to control prices and expose them to the free play of the market place at the same time.

The market won a Pyrrhic victory against the controllers. When the New Economic Model became fully operative in 1967, it started running into trouble straightaway. Surveying the first round of reform in action Professor Šik stated that wholesale prices had risen by 29 per cent instead of the planned 19 per cent. The market remained a seller's market, the economy was still one of scarcity. (*Nová Mysl*, 14 April 1967.) In May 1967 in the Belgrade newspaper *Politika* Professor Šik complained about the slowness in the implementation of economic reforms in Czechoslovakia. 'My plan ... is being tried out only in some enterprises and little things. The resistance to it becomes ever sharper and more evil. Of course we can go on playing about, but tomorrow the government will be compelled to introduce the system by force. There will be no other way.'

The economic situation was explosive. Many people maintained that the new model changed nothing and that it would be preferable to return to the old ways. Professor Šik's reforms came to be regarded as yet another attempt at tinkering with the economy, without any social or political significance, the kind of meaningless activity people were used to from the past.

The Czechs and the Slovaks had many reasons to be dispirited. In comparison with other countries they have done very badly indeed. One of their economists (Otto Schmidt in *Literární Listy*, 23 May 1968) has calculated that the average industrial wage in Czechoslovakia was 1,448 (calculated in Czech crown units on the basis of 1964 U.N. statistics) as compared with:

France   2,250
Austria   2,250

West Germany 3,560
U.K. 4,170
Sweden 5,900
U.S.A. 10,400

while the average monthly salary of qualified technical and scientific personnel was:

Czechoslovakia 2,000
France 12,900
U.S.A. 21,000

But the twist came in the comparison of participation, between France and Czechoslovakia, in total world industrial output. In 1962 Czechoslovakia's participation was 1·86 per cent, that of France 3·86 per cent. France had 3·4 times as many inhabitants; Czechoslovakia therefore produced, in absolute terms, 1·75 times more industrial goods. One economist attributed the discrepancy to the 'pathological ultimate ineffectiveness of our production, caused mainly by badly qualified, dilettante management', another added to it the 'complications arising out of our foreign exchange rate'.

Czech foreign trade had been largely East-orientated for many years, and it would not be surprising if the Czechs felt like championship players who have been forced to play beginners only. The stimulus of competition by highly industrialized countries was missing. In addition, they began to suspect that they were losing money on their foreign trade. They certainly had little else than non-convertible rubles to show for it. There was a chronic shortage in Prague of hard currencies for the purchase of capital equipment and other goods in the West.

Towards the end of 1966, for instance, some particulars of the Soviet-Czechoslovak oil agreement, concluded in Moscow in September, were published. Compared with the prices obtaining on the world market, the Czechs thought they might have to pay too much – about twice the world market price – for Russian oil. The Russians will start supplying the Czechs with oil, under the new agreement, in 1970, to the amount of 5 million tons. The Czechs have undertaken to supply machinery and other equipment for the construction of oil fields at Tiumen in western Siberia. They will go on delivering the supplies until 1974, and their value will be over 4,000 million crowns. At that rate, the Czechs will be paying the Russians 18 rubles for a ton of oil, exactly twice the *highest* amount the Germans, the Italians and the Japanese pay in the Soviet Union.

Full convertibility of the crown, together with internal economic reform, were the main tasks before the Czechoslovak economy. The reform had been jeopardized in 1967 because it was not accompanied by political change; the political changes in 1968 were greatly aided because their objectives had been mapped out. The thoughtful, articulate nature of the political upheaval in Czechoslovakia prevented it from taking on the forms of violence.

6. Reform and the Central Committee

At 9 p.m. on 5 January 1968 all Czechoslovak broadcasting stations carried the announcement that Antonín Novotný was replaced by Alexander Dubček as the first secretary of the Communist Party. Since the end of the summer of 1967 indications of sharp conflict on the highest level of the party had been received intermittently, like distress signals from a sinking ship.

The struggle between the conservatives and the reformers reactivated the central committee, and went on simultaneously in the committee and the praesidium. (Since the thirteenth party congress in 1966, the composition of the committee began to change, with local organizations becoming better represented on it than the central party and state organs.) The Jugoslav press agency described the central committee meeting in Prague on 30 and 31 October as 'perhaps the most important one in the last decade'; the Czechoslovak media were less communicative than usual.

The conflict between the conservatives and the reformers revolved around the state of the economy and the role of the party. Novotný and the conservatives defended the old system. They saw the 'leading role of the party' in comprehensive, paternalist terms. The party, bound by strict discipline, was to retain the monopoly of power. The reformers, on the other hand, disapproved of the high claims made for the party, and argued that they were based on the wrong premises. The party was out of touch with the people. Its leaders were ill-informed and uninterested in the political situation in the country: if they continued to disregard it, the party would run the risk of losing its leading position. If they wanted to retain it, they would have to find out what people wanted. The discussions were interrupted in the morning on 31 October: in the afternoon, there was an official celebration of the fiftieth anniversary of the Bolshevik revolution. On the following day Novotný and a few hand-picked friends left for Moscow, to take part in the Soviet festivities.

The opposition to Novotný crystallized around Alexander Dubček, a member of the praesidium and the first secretary of the Slovak Communist Party. They at first attempted to strip Novotný of some of his powers by suggesting that his two functions, in the party and in the state, should be divided. The proposal was bitterly contested. Novotný's partisans maintained that the party should wait until the elections in 1968, and that the President might then give up his office and retain his function as the first secretary of the party. It was a good attempt, by the conservatives, at pretending to misunderstand the situation. The secretaryship was in fact at stake, immediately, and not the President's office in the distant future.

Hard pressed, Novotný played his last trump cards, Soviet support and the Czechoslovak army, in that order. On 8 December 1967 the Soviet first secretary, Leonid Brezhnev, arrived in Prague unexpectedly, on a flying visit. Though Hendrych later remarked that the visit was 'in the nature of an intervention in favour of comrade Novotný', the Czech and Slovak party leaders soon found out that Brezhnev would not exert himself on Novotný's behalf. Brezhnev left Prague on Saturday 9 December, after a farewell dinner given by the praesidium.

When Brezhnev left Prague the praesidium was still divided; the central committee meeting, which was to take place the following week, had to be postponed. Novotný started taking precautions. Miroslav Mamula, head of the party security section with extensive powers over the state and legal machinery, received instructions to compile a list of Novotný's chief opponents and draw up warrants for their arrest. The army was put on the alert, and there was a partial mobilization of the reservists.

After Brezhnev's visit, the mood in Prague was tense. Shortly before midnight on 21 December 1967 an announcement was made that the central committee had been in session since 19 December. The praesidium was meeting at the same time, whenever its members were able to get away from the central committee. It was unable to agree whether Novotný should go and, if he should, who his successor should be. Of the ten members of the praesidium, Otokar Šimůnek, the Czechoslovak representative on Comecon, the east European communist common market, Bohuslav Laštovička, the chairman of the National Assembly and Jiří Hendrych gave Novotný consistent support. Alexander Dubček, Oldřich Černík, Drahomír Kolder and Jaromír Dolanský were opposed to Novotný. The other two Slovak members of the praesidium, Michal Chudík, the chairman of the Slovak National Council, was a Novotný supporter and personally opposed to Dubček; Josef Lenárt, the Prime Minister, had come to Prague in 1963 with the reputation of a reformer, but had done a lot to lose it since. Although Lenárt in the end supported Dubček, he knew that if another Slovak reached a high position in the party or the state, he would lose his.

No agreement was reached in December, and the members of the praesidium and central committee broke off their meetings for the Christmas and New Year celebrations. When they reassembled on 2 January it took them three days to replace Novotný. At one of the final meetings of the praesidium Novotný apparently antagonized Jiří Hendrych, one of his most loyal partisans. The way he did so sounded true to form. Throughout 1967 Hendrych could be found on the most exposed positions of the old guard. He had a lot of opportunities to make himself unpopular, and he took them all. It may have occurred to Novotný that Hendrych had further uses. In the summer of 1967 when the young writer Jan Beneš was tried for his connexions with the Czech emigré newspaper in Paris, *Svědectví*, the police came across the name of Hendrych's daughter, who allegedly was supplying material to the same address. Though no charge was made, Novotný at one of the meetings of the praesidium turned to Hendrych and said, 'I know what your daughter has been up to, Hendrych – she's been sending stuff to *Svědectví*.' Hendrych apparently shouted back, angrily, 'Antonín, you'll never succeed in making another Barák out of me!' (*Sunday Telegraph*, 5 May 1968: see above, page 35.) Hendrych would have made a good scapegoat. (At the congress in June 1967 Hendrych, in shirt-sleeves and braces, unable to make any impression on the writers, making emotional scenes, had the crumpled, defenceless quality about him of politicians down on their luck.) Though difficult to verify, the story has an authentic ring about it.

After the incident in the praesidium, Novotný lost Hendrych's support. The deadlock was broken. Alexander Dubček was the strongest candidate for Novotný's succession. He had been the chief spokesman of the reformers since the October 1967 central committee plenum, and his final emergence as the party leader early in January testified to the nature of the conflict. It was no palace revolution, no personal reshuffle caused by a switch in the alliances within the praesidium. It was a conflict of two different views of the party and the state. Dubček did not seek the support of his two fellow Slovaks in the praesidium because in that way he would have weakened his position as the leading protagonist of reform. He received solid backing from the Slovaks on the central committee.

Alexander Dubček was born at a small Slovak town, Uhrovec, on 27 November 1921. His parents had returned from America three months before. His father, now the head of the Slovak Academy, had been a founder member of the

'Socialist Party of Illinois'. In 1925 the Dubčeks moved to the Soviet Union. Young Alexander was apprenticed as a pattern maker there, and the family returned to Slovakia shortly before the outbreak of the war. Alexander joined the Communist Party in 1939 and, as a worker at the Škoda factory at Dubnice, was a member of the party's illegal organization. He was wounded twice in the Slovak rising, in which his American-born brother Julius was killed in January 1945. After the end of the war, Dubček worked for four years at a factory in Trenčín and in 1949 became a full-time party functionary. After two years as the leading secretary of the district party committee at Trenčín, he moved to Bratislava, the Slovak party capital, and from there, in 1953, to Banská Bystrica. Between 1955 and 1958 he attended the party school in Moscow where he graduated with distinction. On his return to Bratislava he became the leading secretary of the district committee, and a member of the two central committees, in Bratislava and Prague. At that point Dubček started rising to prominence. In 1960 he was elected a secretary of the central committee of the Czechoslovak party; in 1962 he became a member of the praesidium and in the following year, the first secretary of the Communist Party of Slovakia.

A modest person, Dubček lived with his wife and three sons at a small house near Bratislava. He had a reputation in the party for 'clean hands'; he refused, for instance, to endorse the treatment of the Czech writers by the party in September 1967. For a few months after his appointment in January 1968 Dubček had a makeshift room at a hotel, probably wanting to make certain that he would stay in Prague. He represents a new type of communist politician. In comparison with Novotný, his public *persona* has an infinitely lighter touch. His speeches are discursive, almost free from jargon; he occasionally slows down, searches for the right expression, and he knows how to please. He delighted his listeners in Prague when he told them how glad he was that he had become a citizen of that town at last. The gloomy paternalism has little place in Dubček's politics. His message is lighter, and lightly delivered. Dubček is ready to listen to people and take advice. Its quality will matter.

Dubček's 'national' communism, the comparatively high degree of independence from Moscow, is in tune with the developments in the socialist countries of eastern Europe since 1956. Its origins may be traced to the Second World War. In the first decade after its end, the degree of dependence of the east European communist parties on the Soviet Union was related to the amount of aid from Russia the party had received on its way to power. Tito, at the head of a strong partisan movement in Jugoslavia, could afford to be independent; Wilhelm Pieck and Ulbricht in East Germany very much less so.

Gottwald in Prague was not bound in the same way, yet. The whole pre-war development of Soviet communism was concentrated into his five years in power, between 1948 and 1953. Opening hopefully with a 'socialist' revolution that made the Communist Party the decisive political factor in the country, Gottwald died in the middle of the great Prague purges. The charges against the chief defendants at the Prague trials in 1952 and 1954, of 'Titoist revisionism' in Slánský's case and of 'Slovak nationalism' in the case of Clementis, were finally resolved in the struggle between Dubček and Novotný.

To the Slovaks, Stalinism was presented in the form of Prague centralism, and in that way the habit of independence came easier to them than to the Czechs. Dubček, with his distinguished record in the Slovak rising, without the experience of wartime exile in Stalin's Russia, can deal with the Russians as an equal. The dates of his study at the Moscow party school are also important. In the years 1955–8 Khrushchev put an end to the cult of personality and loosened the ties that bound together Stalin's empire in eastern Europe.

Dubček is tough and has a political programme. So far his

tactics have been impeccable. He and his supporters had made the pace in the crisis without making any tactical compromises. At the critical moment in December 1967 Dubček and General Prchlík summoned a meeting of high-ranking officers to the party political school in Prague. Special representatives were dispatched to army commands throughout the country, and they prevented Novotný and General Janko, the deputy Minister of Defence, from using the army for their own purposes. With the army and the majority of the central committee behind Dubček, the warrants made out for his own and his supporters' arrests were useless.

At its meetings early in January, the central committee elected four new members to the praesidium. They were all Dubček's men. Jan Pillar, originally a metal turner, who joined the party in 1945, had risen high in the party hierarchy. He was switched by Novotný from the party to the government, became deputy Prime Minister in 1962 and was demoted in 1965. From then until January 1968 he occupied the comparatively humble post of the deputy Minister of Heavy Industry. Josef Špaček, the youngest member of the praesidium (born in 1927), a graduate of the party college in Prague, had been the ideological, and since April 1966, the first secretary in the Brno district. He had protected the outspoken Brno literary journal, *Host do domu,* and took a decisive stand against Novotný in the party crisis. Josef Borůvka, a pre-war member of the Communist Party, a colourful, fast-talking chairman of a farmers' cooperative in north-eastern Bohemia, asked for permission to stay at his village when he was elected to the praesidium. The fourth new member was Emil Rigo, the head of the party organization at the large East Slovak Iron Foundry. Later in January, personal changes in the Slovak party were announced. Vasil Bilak succeeded Dubček as the first secretary.

Otherwise, a curious peace descended on public life in Czechoslovakia after the announcement, on 5 January 1968,

of the result of the struggle at the top. The politicians seemed
to have all energy drained out of them. Active political life
was resumed towards the end of the month. On 29 January
Dubček arrived on a brief visit in Moscow. He assured the
Russians that the personal changes in Prague would not interfere with the east European diplomatic and military systems,
and that a Czechoslovak delegation would attend the meeting
of the communist parties in Budapest planned for the end of
the month. He asked the Soviet leaders to let the Czechs and
the Slovaks sort out their own affairs. Before Dubček left for
Moscow, a foreign affairs commentator on the Czech party
daily had stressed the independence and sovereignty of all
communist parties. On 4 February at Komarno, a border
town between Slovakia and Hungary, Dubček met Kadar,
the Hungarian party leader, and assured him that all was well
in Czechoslovakia; three days later, at Moravská Ostrava,
near the Moravian–Polish frontier, Dubček talked to Gomulka
on the same subject. On 19 February Vladimír Koucký, the
secretary of the central committee in charge of relations with
foreign communist countries, left for Rumania.

Having made certain of support, or at least of benevolent
neutrality, on the part of the influential communist leaders in
eastern Europe, Dubček turned to internal problems. A few
of his prominent comrades were getting impatient. Early in
February Gustav Husák, who had been given a life sentence in
1954 as a Slovak 'bourgeois nationalist' and who was rehabilitated in 1963, wrote that people were watching the new
situation with new hopes but also with old scepticism. (*Kul-
túrny Život*, 2 February 1968.) Miloslav Galuška, the former
ambassador to London, said on Prague radio that he remembered a similar occasion, in 1956. Everybody in the party then
talked 'openly and frankly', and all for nothing.

The slow pace made by Dubček was, however, well suited
to the situation. There was no point in passing the word
round that the first secretary was prepared to go far in the

direction of reform. It might have been misunderstood. For his own part, Dubček wanted to find out what kind of demands would be made.

In the meanwhile, the first casualties at the top of the party apparatus were announced. Miroslav Mamula, in charge of security, was the first to go, to a job as a clerk in the aircraft factory at Letňany. He was replaced by Colonel-General Václav Prchlík. The army's political adviser since 1956, he became a member of the central committee in 1958, and a deputy of the National Assembly in 1960. He had helped to prevent Novotný from using the army against the reformers. Prchlík was succeeded at the army's political centre by Major-General Egyd Pepich, originally a steelworker who had fought in the Slovak uprising and became, after the war, a career officer. Hendrych was dislodged early in March, and Josef Špaček, the newly elected member of the party praesidium, was put in charge of ideology.

At the twentieth anniversary of the communist take-over of power, on 22 February 1968, with east European and Russian party leaders present, Dubček made his first major speech. He appealed to all Czechs and Slovaks to help him draw the country out of its crusty apathy. He told the workers that he was relying especially on their cooperation, and added that the key to the solution of the current problems was political. He stressed the need for full rehabilitation of former political prisoners, of people who had suffered under the old regime, especially of all those who had 'worked for the Republic in the First and the Second World Wars'. He criticized the 1960 constitution in regard to the nationality question, and said that a new arrangement, acceptable not only to the Slovaks but also to the Czechs, would have to be worked out. On foreign affairs, Dubček said that Czechoslovakia's main area of interest was Europe, and his reference to West Germany sounded relatively mild, in contrast to Gomulka's and Ulbricht's cliché descriptions of West German 'militarism and revanchism'. Brezhnev then praised Czechoslovakia for its struggle against 'nationalism' and for its past achievements: a reminder to Dubček where Soviet sympathies really lay. The same theme was elaborated on by President Novotný, in his address to a mass rally on the following day. The customary military parade did not take place.

At the time of the anniversary celebrations, the Czechoslovak army weekly published an article by the new head of the Army Political Headquarters, General Pepich, confirming the reports that Novotný had attempted, at the turn of the year, a military *coup*. (*Obrana Lidu*, 23 February 1968.) Two days later, on 25 February 1968, Major-General Jan Šejna crossed the Czechoslovak-Hungarian border, together with his 18-year-old son and a young girl, and the Hungarian and Jugoslav authorities were asked for help in establishing his whereabouts. Šejna, as the secretary of the party committee in the Ministry of Defence, was directly subordinated to Mamula, the security head in the central committee. A very young general – Šejna was born in 1927 – a farm worker by original profession, he was a candidate member of the central committee and a deputy of the National Assembly. The party seconded Šejna to the army, and he rose fast through the commissioned ranks. Careworn and shy, Šejna became interested in writing sometime in 1963. He was then a full colonel. He found tutors to teach him to write, and new friends from the literary and film world. Antonín Novotný, the President's son and managing director of *Artia*, the international publishing house in Prague, was among them.

In December 1967 President Novotný asked Šejna to make certain of army support. Šejna cooperated with Colonel-General Vladimír Janko, deputy Minister of Defence, and it seems that they ordered the army alert, and began moving the first tank division, based in western Bohemia, towards Prague. The role of General Lomský, the Minister of Defence, in the affair is not quite clear. At peak viewing time early in March

1968, in the interval of a televized broadcast of an ice-hockey match, General Lomský denied his complicity in the plot. He said that the army had made no attempt to influence the deliberations of the central committee, and added that suspicions may have arisen as a result of military manoeuvres between 4 and 18 December in central, northern and western Bohemia, and that someone may have tried to 'give an order for the abuse of the armed forces behind my back'.

Šejna and Janko, the chief plotters, did not make a good team. Janko was an experienced career officer, who had fought in the Czechoslovak division on the Russian front during the war. When he returned home he became, at thirty-three, the youngest of the generals. Šejna, on the other hand, had no military experience worth speaking of. He failed Novotný because he had not made certain where the loyalty of the regional commanding officers lay. Šejna's escape at the end of February 1968 ruled out the survival of Novotný in the office of President but, at the same time, it put Dubček and his friends into an unenviable position. Šejna was the highest-ranking officer ever to escape from any of the Warsaw Pact countries, and his flight must have caused a lot of headaches among the commanders of the Pact forces. The defection gave Czechoslovakia's allies an excuse by which they could exert pressure against the reformers in Prague, especially in military matters.

Nevertheless, the official explanation of Šejna's escape – large scale manipulation with clover seed – made a small contribution to the gaiety of nations. Ray S. Cline, the CIA boss in West Germany, had the biggest *coup* on his hands since 1962, when he had put photographs of the Cuban missile sites before President Kennedy. The last act of the generals' plot took place on 14 March 1968, when General Janko shot himself in his official car. It was the first of the few shots fired in the revolution.

Though he had lost every round including the last but one,

Novotný did not concede defeat on 5 January 1968. He was not content to remain the titular head of the state. He knew that the January changes had failed to affect the basic structure of the party and the dispositions between it and the state: he knew that the majority of the people to whom he had given appointments were still in their jobs. He overestimated their personal loyalty to himself, and underestimated the appeal of the reformers' platform. In order to repair his damaged position, Novotný made a bid to rally the workers behind him. On 17 February he visited the Č K D, the biggest industrial plant in the eastern suburbs of Prague, on which he had always lavished attention. His stereotype speech – on the past achievements of his government and the new threat to the interests of the working class – was mildly acclaimed.

In that way Novotný helped the cause of reform. He forced the debate into the factories, into the open air of public life. It did not remain a matter concerning a few people at the top of the party hierarchy, but became the concern of the whole people. A dialogue between the rulers and the ruled was started, and the revolution was daily renewed. After twenty years' silence, the conversation became a compulsive necessity.

Instead of manning the barricades, the Czechs and the Slovaks listened, watched and read. There was no need for anyone to march and occupy the centres of communications. They stood at the disposal of the people who wanted to use them. Editorial offices and broadcasting studios became the focal points of the revolution. A new kind of politician emerged. The apparatus of the party was thrown into the melting-pot, and the highest prizes did not go to the people who could manipulate the apparatus, but to those who could capture and hold the attention of a mass audience. The reformers themselves were astonished by the flood they had released.

Intensely political brains-trusts became the most popular pastime. In March and April 1968 hundreds of them took place all over Czechoslovakia. The first one was arranged by the Prague organization of the youth movement and by the historical institute of the Communist Party on Wednesday 13 March 1968. The meeting took place in one of the large dance halls in the centre of Prague; several hundreds of young people got in. Many thousands had to stay out, and the overflow stopped the traffic in the streets outside. The success of the first meeting convinced its organizers that another one was needed. It was held a week later, in the largest assembly hall available. The Congress Palace was designed to accommodate 3,000, and at least twice as many young people got in. Every square foot of the floor was filled. The little sales kiosks were used as additional accommodation; the young people themselves looked after the lighting of the hall. They trained the strongest spotlights on the speakers: the chairman asked for them to be turned off. Outside the hall, large groups of people listened to the proceedings on their transistor sets. They were an hour behind; the meeting had been opened at 7, and the full recorded broadcast began at 8 p.m. The two meetings were intended to 'open the door' in politics and make information available on matters of public interest.

Josef Smrkovský, now the chairman of the National Assembly, was one of the brightest stars of those public meetings. Born in 1911, Smrkovský went on from school to become an apprentice baker. He joined the party in 1933 and received his political schooling in the Soviet Union. He worked in the communist youth organization before the war; in 1944 he became a member of the central committee of the illegal Communist Party. He played an important role in the anti-German uprising in Prague in May 1945, and in 1948 became the deputy Minister of Agriculture. He was arrested in August 1951 and his name came up in the Slánský trial, when he was described as 'an agent of the Gestapo'. After his release in 1955 Smrkovský remained, for eight years, in the wilderness. He had a job in forest administration, and then on a collective farm; he was officially rehabilitated in 1963 and became a member of the agricultural section of the central committee, and in January 1967 the Minister of Forestry.

Smrkovský has a pleasant public manner which combines enthusiasm and a light touch; he has a reflective, retrospective turn of mind. He made a strong appeal to his young audience. He told them, '... you have the right and the duty to be more radical and more revolutionary. We older people have to see to it that during this great transformation of our country, of our state, nothing happens that would mean a catastrophe.' The questions covered everything from political to personal topics. Most of them were serious and straight; some were frivolous, and had a sting in the tail. A writer, Jan Procházka, was asked, 'What do you think of Jiří Hendrych?' Procházka replied, 'He is a very interesting literary figure.' There was an agony column question: 'My husband is an officer and a Slovak and at the place where I work everybody gives me hell. What should I do?' Procházka's answer was, 'We all have our problems.' A personal question elicited a political reply: 'Is it true that Antonín Novotný became your son's godfather last year?' 'It was not a son but a daughter, and he was not her godfather but he came to dinner one night. He came to dinner because last year I felt like influencing the course of European history. A West German journalist rang me up because he wanted to say something important, we met and he told me that Herr Kiesinger should like to send a message to Mr Novotný. So I asked comrade Novotný to dinner. He came, I gave him the message, and nothing happened.'

Rehabilitation of people unjustly sentenced on political charges was one of the overriding interests of the audience. The inquiries addressed to Marie Švermová, one of the founders of the Communist Party, largely concerned that problem. As she was reading the questions addressed to her, Švermová later said, 'I wondered why young people, who had not lived through the dark period of the 1950s, should talk about rehabilitation, why do they return to those questions? I can explain it only by their desire to clear the decks.' To the question of the causes of the great purges, Švermová replied,

It is a question that we used to put to ourselves and that staggered us at first. We had a lot of time to consider those questions. And believe me, that it took long before we got down to the causes, to the beginnings, how was it possible that one communist fought another, that old friends no longer trusted each other, that they were afraid of one another. The following years I was not a member of society, I was isolated from it. And believe me that I often said to myself – after my release from prison – that I had been better off in prison than living at a time when people, in a tremendously strained atmosphere, under psychological pressure, demanded a sentence, a sentence of death, for all those who had been described as criminals. I cannot unfold here for you all those events, they did not begin one day, it was a long development. The whole period will have to be examined. I believe that it began with the acceptance of a number of incorrect dogmas of Stalin, including his view about the immediate danger of war. In that period the endeavour began to discover the hidden enemy, all those who could form a fifth column, in the event of war. In the end the search went on in our own party, under the slogan that the enemy was trying to infiltrate the party, including the top positions.

Marie Švermová knew the post-war leaders of the party well, and she thought that Klement Gottwald must have become a victim himself, that he believed all 'those monstrous accusations and withdrew his protection from his closest friends. When he stopped believing 'them [the accusations] he could not go on living.' Gottwald died three days after his return to Prague from Stalin's funeral.

The most sensitive question – Czechoslovakia's relationship with the Soviet Union – was answered by Smrkovský:

Comrade Brezhnev was here, he was asked before Christmas, and when he was told what was going on here he said, 'That is, comrades, your Czechoslovak affair and the Soviet party and the

Soviet Union will not interfere in your internal affairs.' That happens to be the truth. . . . When we got to know that comrade Brezhnev had been asked, that he was here, we were apprehensive as to why he was here. When we got to know what his point of view was – he arrived in the morning and got on the plane in the evening – we were very happy. Many of you of course may think that the relationship between us and the Soviet Union is not one of equals. It's because you have taken no interest in politics, you have been interested in politics for two months only. You thought that here, in our Republic, the Soviet Union was in the driver's seat. If anyone is still thinking that, my young friends, he's terribly wrong. Those times are behind us. Comrades, our relations are now built on the principle of equality, on the principle of sovereignty. That's the truth. . . . We see very often young people giving way – especially at ice-hockey matches – to their dislike of the Soviet Union. Well, look here, to love, not to love, that's everybody's private affair. Nobody can force that on you. But you must think over this one fact: look at the map, when you go back to school, or at home, look at the frontier, who our neighbour is, because we must now live politically, it may interest you, what kind of politics go on there, on the other side, in Germany. So that you would not live through a frightful disenchantment, something we ourselves had lived through. Don't take it lightly what I'm saying now and don't play around, don't underestimate your responsibility for the safety of our state. I should like to add that if it were not for the Soviet Union I would be afraid for the future of our country. I say that sincerely. And for our various sins, doing everything after the 'example of the Soviet Union', cleaning one's teeth that way and so on, for that, the Soviet Union is not responsible . . .

At the second meeting with young people, on 20 March 1968, Smrkovský warned them against *agents provocateurs* in the audience, especially on their way home, so they would not get into scuffles with the police. He reminded the audience that the debate should not be 'barren or lapse into some unmanageable anarchy, for which we all would have to pay'. It should be a forward-looking discussion; Smrkovský added that, 'Nowadays many of us, I think, realize that our country

may be able to become a type of socialist state that would
have a lot to say to the people of the developed countries of
the European West.'

The meeting in the big hall of the Congress Palace turned
out to be a good-humoured occasion. It went on for six hours.
The speakers – Professors Šik and Goldstücker, Jiří Hanzelka, the author and traveller, and a number of others –
dealt with the questions before them openly and briskly.
Luboš Holeček, who had been expelled from the university
the year before, appeared on the platform in his army uniform.
The question of monopoly of power was, Holeček said, of
first-rate importance, and he went on,

> If it is a tremendous advance today that we can speak and meet in
> this way, we realize that our present voice in support of the party,
> led, or represented by comrade Dubček, is not our final demand or
> our last word. In this situation we shall behave wisely, deliberately
> and humanely, and we shall not let this progress, with its confused
> and accidental beginnings, be spoilt in any way, and we declare at
> the same time that we shall work for and carry out our own pro-
> gramme, the programme of young people, which perhaps will not be
> identical with the plans of someone as distinguished and progressive
> as, say, Professor Goldstücker.

After six hours full of excitement a message to the National
Assembly was drafted in the name of the meeting, demanding
the resignation of President Novotný, as well as a 'manifesto
of young people'. It stated that return to capitalist order was
out of the question because 'socialism is a fact in our country'.
But what kind of socialism? The abolition of the monopoly
of power and information was an essential premise for the
'thorough-going democratization of public life'. The young
people demanded the abolition of censorship, revision of the
law on assembly, changes in the way passports and exit
visas were issued, economic reforms and the 'whole truth
about our economy', as well as 'legal guarantees of democracy'.
The manifesto envisaged the setting up of a 'constitutional

court' which would look after harmony between the laws and the constitution, and after the publication of new laws. A demand was made for the separation of the legislative, executive and judicial powers, and for the rehabilitation of all unjustly sentenced citizens. 'We want our foreign policy to go on taking into account the geographical position of the Republic in Central Europe.' After the resolution had been read, a lively and sometimes sharp debate on foreign affairs took place. In the end, the original sentence was accepted with the addition: '... and to establish equal relations with the socialist countries, especially the Soviet Union.'

7. The April Action Programme

Throughout March, pressure from below continued to build up. Two anniversaries – of Thomas Masaryk's birth on 7 March and Jan Masaryk's death three days later – gave the Czechs an opportunity to claim the inheritance that Novotný's regime had denied them. Official delegations and thousands of students and workers visited the village cemetery at Lány where father and son are buried. At the same time, top functionaries who had been too closely connected with the Novotný system came under severe pressure in their own party. District party conferences criticized a number of Ministers, including Lenárt, the Premier, Bohuslav Laštovička, the chairman of the National Assembly, and Martin Vaculík, the first secretary of Prague district. Vaculík, who accepted an invitation to answer questions at the philosophical faculty of Prague University, was told, 'Don't be afraid, Mr Vaculík, with your vocabulary you will be able to survive several revolutions.'

The last visible link with the old regime snapped when Novotný resigned, on 22 March 1968, the office of the President. The party praesidium recommended General Ludvík Svoboda to succeed him. The National Assembly accepted the recommendation, by a secret ballot, on 30 March. Ludvík Svoboda had fought on the Russian side in the two world wars, in the Czech Legion in the first and as a commander of the Czechoslovak Army Corps in the second. In April 1945 Beneš appointed Svoboda the Minister of Defence. He joined the Communist Party in 1948 and in March 1950 he left the army, on Stalin's direct order. He was then in charge, for over a year, of the state sports organization and, early in 1952, disappeared from public life altogether. He was imprisoned for a short time and then worked as an accountant of an agricultural cooperative. On one of his visits to Prague Khrushchev inquired about Svoboda, and it took some time before he was located. Since then Svoboda had been slowly re-emerging in public life, as a writer of articles on military matters. In November 1965 he was awarded the titles of Hero of the Soviet Union and Hero of the Czechoslovak Socialist Republic. He is now seventy-two years old, spry, and a figurehead of the new regime.

The crucial plenum of the central committee which opened at the Prague Castle on 28 March was interrupted for the election of the President. It approved Dubček's recommendation of the presidential candidate, accepted the resignation of Novotný from the praesidium and elected Josef Smrkovský to the vacated seat. Dr Čestmír Císař, who had run into trouble with Novotný and was serving as the ambassador to Rumania at the time of the January changes, was elected a secretary of the central committee in charge of education and science. When the central committee reassembled on Monday 1 April 1968 Dubček and his allies started straightaway treating the committee with respect. Its proceedings were given extensive publicity.

Dubček told the members of the committee that their main task was to discuss the action programme, a draft of which they had before them. The situation since January 1968 and the role of the party were the two topics Dubček returned to again and again in his speech. He said that the committee members in particular were aware 'how much we differed in January', and that, when the leadership of the party 'opened the door to the new developments and took the lead, it could have no detailed plan as to how these events would unfold'. The spontaneous way in which the situation developed, the way in which it was not manipulated, were its main merits.

Many people have been taken by surprise to such an extent that they are expressing fears whether the party is not giving way to pressures, whether it will not give up its positions, if it is not being pushed by these developments, and whether it will be able to deal with incorrect attitudes and harmful demands which always occur in that kind of process.

Dubček was aware that many people in the party might prefer the old certainties when 'one seemingly undifferentiated social interest, corresponding to the ideas of some of our leading comrades' was in existence rather than 'the enormous amount of differentiated and opposing interests and attitudes, representing certain short- and long-term interests of the most varied social groups', that had come to the surface since January. He added that, 'resuscitation of certain nonsocialist moods, even angry cries for revenge' had taken place, and that the party 'must not be jumped into legalizing those moods under the cover of democracy and rehabilitation'. Nevertheless, Dubček said, 'Let's not be afraid of this wave but let's learn from it.' The party would have to analyse and lead it. 'Confidence in the party, and, inside the party, self-confidence, are growing.'

Dubček placed Stalin's policies against the background of 'intensified antagonisms between the socialist and the capitalist systems' or, in other words, the beginnings of the cold war. In April 1968 the first secretary of the Czechoslovak Communist Party saw its task as 'the realization of the new phase of socialist revolution in the epoch of non-antagonistic relations' leading to the 'need to develop, shape and create a political system that would correspond to the new situation'. The party had to develop creatively the revolutionary programme of Marxist socialism.

Because of the scientific theory with which the party is equipped, because of the party's historical achievements, because the process of reform and the entry into the next stage of development of our country is being accomplished under the auspices of the party, we think that we have the right to declare, with a better justification than ever: the Communist Party goes on being the decisive, organized, progressive force in our society.

The party, according to Dubček, should make a powerful impact on society but it must not rule that society by force. It will have to defend its leading position in public discussion: 'authority must be renewed, it's never given to anyone once and for all.' Dubček then discussed the tasks of the government and its relationship with the National Assembly, and he said that all representative bodies, up to the level of the Assembly, should become places where decisions were really made. Dubček saw his new type of 'socialist democracy' as resting on the revival of representative bodies and real independence of all 'social and interest organizations'. It was, he said, not a question of the 'revival of party life of formal parliamentarianism'. Dubček recommended the cancellation of the decision made by the committee in September 1967 to transfer the direction of the Writers' Union weekly to the Ministry of Culture, and to expel from the party the three writers, Klíma, Liehm and Vaculík. He also asked for the withdrawal of the reprimand of Pavel Kohout, the writer and dramatist, and for the scrapping of the disciplinary action against Milan Kundera.

On the following day, 2 April 1968, Jiří Hendrych and Vladimír Koucký resigned all their party functions. (*Rudé Právo*, 2 April 1968.) In his address to the central committee, Koucký, who had been in charge of education at the time of the Strahov incident between the police and students, blamed his sickness at the time and bad briefing: Hendrych, who was more open, said that, 'For the fear for the unity of the party I tried to reconcile extremes that were irreconcilable. That was my worst mistake.' Antonín Novotný spoke, for over an hour, on 4 April. He had no place on the list of speakers, and, in his case, the fifteen-minute limit was waived. 'I should like to say that our path, from the beginning of our national and democratic revolution, was in the main necessary and correct.'

Though he admitted certain small mistakes – Šejna's promotion was one of them – he agreed with

those comrades who say that the party has not got ideological and political processes sufficiently under its control. Various journalists influence the public in the positive or negative sense. Negative forces in the country are being activated. In connexion with rehabilitation, when everything is supposed to be rehabilitated, a campaign has arisen that can do nothing but harm to the party. We must not be confused because everyone says nowadays that he is for socialism. [*Práce*, 6 April 1968]

He was laughed at while speaking, and soon afterwards, historians at the Academy of Sciences sent him an open letter, in reply to the speech. They reminded Novotný that he had reached the top party team in 1951, when the big political trials were being prepared. Though he did not then belong among the chief organizers of the trials, towards the end of the first big wave – in the years 1953 and 1954 – Novotný was at the top of the party hierarchy. He therefore had to bear, with Zápotocký and Široký, the President and the Prime Minister respectively, his share of responsibility. 'In 1956, you were aware, together with other members of party leadership, that the trials had been engineered. Such knowledge should have been followed by decisive action. It took place only after eight years, under a great pressure of circumstances.' Nor did the historians let Novotný get away with the statement that, while he was President, no one was persecuted illegally for his political opinions. Leaving aside the many cases from the years 1956–61, the historians reminded Novotný that, in 1961, a group of old party members and officials were arrested; in 1964 Ivan Sviták, the philosopher with a political turn of mind and with him, the whole philosophical section of the Academy of Sciences was persecuted; in the summer of the same year Dr Purš was arrested.

The historians pointed out, in their letter to the former President, that 'new opportunities for a basic change of policy reappeared after the twenty-second congress of the Soviet Communist Party in 1961'. What was Novotný doing then? He was busy discovering and punishing a group of 'pro-Jugoslav revisionists' and pressing the party intellectuals as hard as he could. The former Slovak Minister of Agriculture Julius Ďuřiš was dropped from the central committee because he disagreed with Novotný's policies. Finally, after the twelfth congress of the Czechoslovak party in 1962 'the development began which you did not oppose in every regard'. The trials of party members were re-examined more thoroughly and the party began considering economic reforms suggested by Oto Šik and others. The political and cultural life of the nation started looking up, but new hopes were again dashed to the ground.

Your attitude in the last year showed that you had chosen extreme instruments of force in order to suppress the movement for democratic reforms of our society. In your speech to the April plenum of the central committee you presented the current developments in the party and in our society as the continuation of something for which you have always, though inconsistently, striven for. Here we disagree with you most profoundly.

On the day of his speech Novotný was formally relieved of his membership of the praesidium and of the secretariat of the central committee. Michal Chudník, Otakar Šimůnek, Jiří Hendrych and Bohuslav Laštovička left the praesidium as well. Miroslav Pastyřík, the former trade union leader, ceased being its candidate member. Dubček then put before the committee a list of the new candidates aiming to cut down the membership of the praesidium as well as the duplication of functions. More men were to hold fewer top jobs. The secret ballot resulted in a few surprises, among them the election of Martin Vaculík and Josef Lenárt, the former Prime Minister, as praesidium candidates: Lenárt also became a secretary to the central committee. The proposal that all communist members of the government should resign was passed. The new cabinet, announced a few days later, was led by Oldřich Černík, Dubček's old ally in the praesidium; Professor Oto Šik became one of his deputies. The first phase of the reform movement was completed.

When the central committee reassembled on 1 April 1968 it appointed a team which was to draft the proposals for the 'action programme' of the party. Oto Šik, Pavel Auersperg and Radovan Richta, the head of the Academy group that had prepared the study *Civilization at the Crossroads* (see above, page 87) were on the team. (Zdeněk Mlynář, head of the other Academy study group, was elected, on 4 April 1968, a member of the party secretariat.) On 5 April, the day of its last meeting, the central committee approved the text of the action programme.

It was strengthened by the long-term considerations that had first appeared in the findings of the Richta study group. It stressed the need to develop creatively the Marxist heritage by placing it into its original context, that of an industrialized society. Its opening paragraph suggested that, 'Social advancement in the Czech lands and in Slovakia has been carried in the twentieth century by the two strongest currents: the national movement of liberation, and socialism.' The conclusion of the programme stated that

We now have to go through unusual situations. We shall experiment, give socialist development new forms, use creative Marxist thinking and the experience of the international workers' movement, rely on the correct understanding of social development in Czechoslovakia. It is a country which bears the responsibility, before the international communist movement, for the evaluation and utilization of its relatively advanced material base, uncommonly high level of education, and undeniable democratic traditions. If we did not use such an opportunity, nobody could ever forgive us. [Action Programme of the Czechoslovak Communist Party, page 29, published as a supplement to *Rudé Právo* on 8 April 1968]

There existed a specifically 'Czechoslovak way to socialism' because it had been the first industrial country to set out on the socialist transformation of its society. After a brief analysis of the causes of the 'deep social crisis', in which the 'extraordinary position of individuals, especially comrade Novotný', was mentioned, the authors of the programme addressed Novotný direct: 'The party decisively condemns the attempts to set individual classes and groups of socialist society against each other, and it will remove every cause creating tensions among them.'

Though the working class would remain the main support of the system, the party would 'make every effort so that complicated and creative work of the mind be justly rewarded'. One section of the programme was devoted to 'false egalitarianism' and its removal. It was seen as

one of the main brakes on intensive economic development and the improvement of the standard of living. Egalitarianism is harmful because it protects lazy good-for-nothings and irresponsible workers against self-sacrificing and industrious people, unqualified against qualified workers, technically and professionally backward men against gifted people with initiative.

In the discussion of the leading role of the party, the programme made a specific mention of the removal of the 'cadre ceiling', i.e. of the practice of excluding non-communists from top jobs in industry, education, etc.

A programme for the fourteenth congress of the party, to take place late in the summer of 1968, and a new constitution would have to be prepared. There was, however, no need to delay reforms. The basic premise for reform was to 'show which organ and which functionary or official is responsible for what, what is the guarantee of reform, whether institutions, methods of work, or particular people have to be changed'. A new definition of the functions of organizations and of individuals, together with the integration of the various organizations into political life, was envisaged as the means for the development of a new 'socialist democracy'. 'The power of the socialist state cannot be monopolized by any single party, or a coalition of political parties, it has to be accessible to all the political organizations of the people.' Socialist democracy must go deeper, the action programme claimed, than bourgeois democracy. Regular employment of public opinion polls and the publication of their results was envisaged. The freedoms of assembly, organization and movement, and protection of minority rights and of personal property was to be guaranteed by law. The Republic should become a state of two equal peoples: the Czechs and the Slovaks. The programme argued that division of power would become a guarantee against its abuse. The organs of the state had been underestimated in the past, and even at government level, there had been the 'tendency to shift responsibility on to the party and get rid of independence in decision-making'.

In its economic part the programme gave full recognition to the efforts of the reformers. It stressed that 'the structure of production must be manifold in the same way as the demands of our market are manifold', and criticized the standard of services. In that sphere there was room for 'small private enterprise'. The economic life of the country should become more elastic, so that it could react swiftly to economic changes at home and abroad. 'The long-term isolation from world markets separated the structure of internal prices from world prices.' Real wages in industry should increase by 2·5 to 3 per cent a year. The trade unions, instead of acting, as they used to do, as a support of the directive economic system, or even as a legislative body, should resume their original functions, and concentrate on the protection of the interests of the working people.

In the section on science and education the programme stated that, 'Socialism originates, maintains itself and wins because of the connexions between the workers' movement and science. ... In the long-term perspective, the victory of socialism over capitalism will be decided on the field of science and technology.' But there were still too many barriers between research and production; the development of social sciences needed the initiative of the party, but the party 'does not interfere with the actual process of creative scientific work'. 'Works of art must not be subjected to censorship', though

The social influence of the arts is not without political significance. We shall take care that freedom of opinion, guaranteed by the constitution, is fully respected. The Communist Party cannot however renounce its task to inspire, and give up the attempt to make works of art help effectively to shape the socialist man in his struggle for the transformation of the world.

In its last part, the programme dealt with foreign policy. The 'world-wide struggle against the forces of imperialist reaction' was mentioned and the necessity of friendly relations with the 'communist and workers' parties of the socialist commonwealth' stressed.

In regard to developed capitalist countries we shall actively pursue the policy of peaceful coexistence. Our geographic situation as well as the needs and opportunities of an industrial country demand a more active European policy aimed at the development of mutually advantageous relations with all the states and international organizations and at the safeguarding of the collective security of the European continent.

The reformers were agreed on the necessity of reviving the country's economy, the abolition of preventive censorship, the need for federal arrangements for Slovakia. But the 'leading' position of the party, and with it closely connected 'guarantees' of the newly won freedom, were more sensitive problems. Until January 1968 only the party leaders had been concerned with its position in the state. In his speech to the central committee on 4 April Novotný made an astute estimate of the deep concern of many of his comrades with the loss of the old certainties. No Communist Party in power had ever allowed an open discussion of its monopoly position.

Under strong pressure, the authors of the April action programme allowed that it was by no means the last word on reform. Though leading communists kept on talking of their country's democratic traditions, they were reluctant to propose the return to some 'formal' multi-party system. They were convinced that the division of state and party functions would mean a considerable advance. Nevertheless, in the new party praesidium two leading reformers – Oldřich Černík and Josef Smrkovský – hold high state offices as well. In the spring 1968 situation, the democratic process would have gone on as long as the Communist Party itself remained democratic. If it restricted the free exchange of opinions in its own organization, if its leaders decided that they want to govern in a different way, the road to the monopoly of power was open before them.

In theory, there exist two other parties in Czechoslovakia. The Socialist Party is a descendant of the National Socialist Party, founded in 1898. Originally established to combat the spread of Marxist socialism, i.e. the influence of the Social Democrat Party, among the Czech workers in Bohemia and Moravia, it became, between the two wars, Dr Edward Beneš's party. The second organization, the People's Party, is related to the traditions of central European Christian socialism. Neither of the two parties extends to Slovakia.

The People's Party had 483,725 members in January 1948; in 1966 their number was down to 21,362. Its newspaper, with a tautology in its title, *Lidová Demokracie* (*Popular Democracy*), prints 156,800 copies on weekdays and 225,000 on Sundays. Until 1956, the party was not allowed to take new members; over a quarter of its membership (26·8 per cent) are pensioners, and 30 per cent are agricultural workers. It has twenty members in the National Assembly and for twenty years it had an excommunicated Catholic priest in the government as the Minister of Health.

The Socialist Party had 652,000 members in 1947, 3,792 in 1949, and 10,705 in 1967. Its daily, *Svobodné Slovo*, prints 170,000 copies on weekdays, 250,000 on Sundays. Their chairman had been the Minister of Justice for twenty years, and they have the same number of deputies as the People's Party – twenty – in the Assembly. At present, they cannot be regarded as serious contenders for political power. They have no programmes and their leaderships, having for long temporized with the old system, have no contribution to make to the new developments. The People's Party newspaper managed to maintain modest standards of daily journalism, but it has been left behind by other newspapers after the relaxation of censorship. Nowadays, while the communist daily tends to quote *The Times*, the Socialist organ still relies on the news and comments in the *Morning Star*. In comparison with the Communist Party the two parties in Bohemia and Moravia, and the other two tiny political organizations in Slovakia, are negligible. Though they have their own machinery and newspapers they are most unlikely to become effective forces in Czechoslovakia's politics. In April 1968 their general secretaries denied that they would make an attempt to build up their parties into mass organizations. (*Student*, 3 and 10 April 1968.)

In the absence of the possibility of revitalizing the old political parties, a variety of views have emerged on how best to reconstruct the checks and balances in a socialist state. One school of thought maintains that public opinion, expressed through the mass media, will be sufficient to control political power. The influence of newspapers and broadcasting, especially television, on the development of political events has been so deep that it set off the suggestion that the mass media should acquire some institutional basis, which would make it possible for them to discharge their political obligations. The mass media would however be doing another job than they are meant to do, and the dissemination of information might again be directly subordinated to political considerations. There would still be no guarantee that the party or the government would take any notice of the points made swiftly and vanishing just as fast on the television screen.

Enlightened members of the Communist Party have argued, on the other hand, that if someone came forward with a genuine alternative programme to their own, he should be given every facility, including organization, for putting it before the people. It was not a genuine political offer. European Marxist socialism had possessed a theory, the basis for a programme, before it started setting up its own organizations. But that was not the customary way. All over Europe, the party has usually come first, and the programme second.

The communists have so far found every other suggestion – mass communications, individual non-party members in the National Assembly or the revival of non-communist parties, political activity by trade unions and other organizations – more acceptable than the proposal for a second party. The idea of an opposition shocked them deeply. (cf. Václav Havel in *Literární Listy*, 4 April 1968.)

It was put to them that competition of views, the alleged basis of democracy, is nothing but its public expression. 'Democracy is not a matter of faith, but of guarantees', and 'public and legal competition for power' is the best guarantee of democracy. 'If the Communist Party does not provide for the fastest development of its effective control from the outside, it will have no guarantee that it will not degenerate at some later time.' The communists have been asked to recognize what the non-communists have known for years: that socialism sacrifices democracy at its own peril.

This is the most sensitive and crucial issue in Czechoslovak politics at the present time, the early summer of 1968. The future of the country may depend on the way it is settled. Though they do not regard their action programme as final, the communist leaders feel that they have gone far enough for the time being. If we contrast the state of the country now with what it was six months ago, they are right. A whole era of historical development has been concentrated into a few months.

8. The Retrospective Revolution

Again and again, the reformers in Prague turned to the past. In a way, it was an historian's revolution. The 'action programme' opened with an historical statement. The Academy historians argued against Novotný's account of his term in power. Writers at their conference in the summer of 1967 analysed their own national past as well as the broader issues of censorship and patronage. On 23 February 1968 the communists celebrated the twentieth anniversary of their take-over of power: 28 October 1968 was the fiftieth anniversary of the foundation of the Czechoslovak Republic.

At one point, however, retrospection became an explosive political issue. Rehabilitation of political prisoners of the 1950s was a part of the look backwards. Many of them are still alive. So are the people who examined them, tortured them and tried them. A former investigator and his victim live at a small summer resort near Prague. One of them has retired, the other has been rehabilitated; both are mentally and physically broken. On sunny days they meet for lunch at a garden restaurant. Such amity is not general.

In Czech historical memory, long periods of adversity are punctuated by tragedy. Enshrined in the legendary beginnings of the nation in the early tenth century there are two murders, one of them a dynastic assassination, the other fratricide: Ludmila, the grandmother of Prince Wenceslas, slain on the orders of her daughter-in-law, Wenceslas murdered by his brother at the door of a church. Ludmila and Wenceslas were later canonized, their short and obscure lives becoming a lasting reproach. When Jan Hus, a follower of Wyclif, a fighter for the reform of the church, a preacher whose sermons touched the imagination of the common people of Prague, the founder of Czech orthography, refused to renounce his teaching before the Council of Constance, he was burnt at the stake, on 6 July 1415, and his ashes were scattered over the river Rhine. Four years later, on 30 July 1419, the first recorded defenestration resulted in riots in Prague, followed by religious wars that lasted some eighteen years. In 1618–20, the opening years of the Thirty Years War, the Czech estates rebelled against the Habsburgs. They were defeated in the battle of the White Mountain on 8 November 1620; on 21 June 1621 twenty-seven leaders of the uprising – three nobles, seven knights and seventeen burghers – were publicly executed in Prague. The Habsburgs held the nation in the palm of their hand. Gradually, the towns were Germanized and the aristocracy de-nationalized; the political centre of the country moved to Vienna; many Czech scholars, who wanted to retain their Protestant religion, went into exile. The victory of the counter-reformation in the Czech lands was complete. Prague became a city of the baroque, the architecture of the counter-reformation. It ceased being a Czech town. The Czechs can now say that the greatest splendour around them reminds them of their greatest national disaster.

They have shared their recent preoccupation with history with the rest of Europe. The department at Prague University is large and has some distinguished internationally known teachers. Books on recent history are immensely popular. Yet the current interest in the past has little to do with an austere academic discipline lacking in general significance, or with the pastimes of the veterans of the Second World War. There is no sentimentality in that retrospection, but a moral problem. The novelists, especially Ludvík Vaculík and Milan Kundera, understood it because they dealt with individual men who were trying, here and now, to come to terms with their past. They were not concerned with some ultimate 'judgement of history' or with the generality of the nation.

The Czechs and the Slovaks are now faced with the same question. They have to come to terms with their past, to stop rejecting large parts of it, and treating them as if they had never happened. The period under review is not very long. It covers the lifetime of one generation. Citizens of the Czechoslovak Republic who are now over fifty years old were all born subjects of the Habsburg Empire. They, and even more so the middle and the young generation, are now faced with their enigmatic past: the Habsburg Empire and its break-up in 1918; the personality and politics of Thomas Masaryk, the founder of the Czechoslovak Republic, and of his friend and aide, Edward Beneš; the Munich crisis in 1938, and the war; the take-over of power by the Communist Party in 1948. They are all surrounded by layers of both hatred and veneration.

The Habsburg Empire was a political and economic reality taken for granted by the parents and grandparents of the present older generation. Above them, there stood the immense patriarchal figure of Franz Josef I. The Czechs were impressed by the court at Vienna and resentful of its remoteness. They usually took a vigorous part in the politics of the empire: sometimes they withdrew into themselves, and refused to play the game any longer.

Under Habsburg auspices, the Czechs had come to life again as a civilized people. In the first half of the nineteenth century, sons of Czech peasants started arriving in large numbers in towns that were German. They won back the foreign towns in their own country for their children. They went to the first Czech schools and their children had, after 1882, a Czech university to go to. It was a shoe-string renaissance. In the middle of the nineteenth century their most popular author spent much of her time writing begging letters because the market for her books was small. The Czechs in Prague collected, penny by penny, the funds to build their national theatre. After the turn of the century the situation changed. A few rich Czechs clubbed together to build their people a large concert hall and ballroom in the middle of Prague. The nation was then prosperous and strong, but it lacked self-confidence and the ultimate proof of its existence: its own state.

Thomas Masaryk became the first professor of philosophy at the Czech University in Prague in 1882. He was thirty-two years old, had an American wife and spoke a kind of Czech which sounded more like Slovak. He was popular with his students, became involved in most of the great public controversies at the time and in 1891 became a deputy in the parliament in Vienna. He had a weakness for writing-paper with a letter of apology printed in copper-plate on its back: it made excuses for the brevity of the hand-written side, pleading pressure of time.

Like most Czech politicians, Masaryk had shown no interest in the break-up of the Habsburg Empire before the First World War. Shortly after its outbreak he went into exile at the age of sixty-four. Masaryk was doubtful of the strength of Russia and convinced that the British Empire had the decisive contribution to make in the war.

Germany and Austria-Hungary had beaten Tsarist Russia before being defeated, in their turn, by Britain and France, reinforced by the United States. The course of those wartime developments made it possible for Masaryk to emerge triumphant at their end.

He had played, in the last stages of the war, the most controversial part of his career. Shortly before the Bolshevik revolution in November 1917 he arranged for the Czech volunteer Legion in Russia, fighting alongside the Russian troops on the eastern front, to become a part of the French army. In the spring of 1918 the Legion got involved in fighting the Bolsheviks along the Trans-Siberian Railway. Some of the Legion troops stayed in Russia until 1920, and were used for the purposes of intervention against Lenin's regime by the western allies.

Under Masaryk and his wartime friend and second-in-command, Edward Beneš, the Czechoslovak Republic became a liberal democratic state. In contrast to the rest of central Europe at the time, it was quite prosperous and quite peaceful. Its nationality policy towards the large German and Hungarian minorities was more sensible than towards the Slovaks (see above, page 71.) But it was a state established at a time when both Germany and Russia, the main contenders for influence in eastern Europe, had been defeated and had withdrawn into themselves. Czechoslovakia was set up under the patronage of the western powers, and its foreign policy was founded on friendship with those powers, especially on the alliance with France.

In their First World War propaganda in the United Kingdom, the United States and France, Masaryk and Beneš had described the Habsburg Empire as a 'prison of nations', in which the Czechs had always suffered and which they had always opposed. Wartime propaganda was accepted and amplified by the Czech historians between the wars. They excised, as far as possible, the Habsburg past from the history of their people, and in that way succeeded in dislodging their history from its central European context. Provisions against the return of the Habsburgs to their former territories and against the union between Austria and Germany were built into the peace treaties. In the years after the First World War the Czechs often acted as if their new state lay just across the river, east of France.

Masaryk resigned the office of President in 1935, and Beneš moved from the Foreign Ministry to the castle. On 14 September 1937 Thomas Masaryk died, in his eighty-seventh year. The whole people went into mourning. Silent queues moved up the hill towards the castle, day and night, when the old man lay in state. A secular canonization took place; a special law was passed by the parliament, recognizing, Roman-style, Masaryk's 'great merit for the state'. The symbol of national independence was dead, and the forces of the enemy were closing in.

A year later, on 29 September 1938, the British, French and Italian Prime Ministers concluded the Munich pact with Hitler. Neither the Soviet Union nor Czechoslovakia were invited to Munich. Czechoslovakia was to surrender to Germany its frontier territories as well as making adjustments in favour of Hungary and Poland. The remainder of Czechoslovakia was guaranteed against 'unprovoked aggression'. The country's former allies had abandoned it, and it relapsed into the central European anarchy created by Hitler with the aid of the German minorities. Its links with western Europe, with middle-class democracy, established only twenty years ago, were broken off.

In March 1939 Hitler occupied Bohemia and Moravia: Slovakia set up on its own, a little state in the shadow of Nazi Germany. After the outbreak of the war in September, thousands of Czechs and Slovaks went into exile. Most of them joined the French and British armed forces. The Communist Party, one of the three biggest political organizations in pre-war Czechoslovakia, had been banned in Bohemia and Moravia, as well as in autonomous Slovakia, in October 1938. It then split into two parts: one in Moscow, the other, illegal, at home. Klement Gottwald, Václav Kopecký and Rudolf Slánský, the pre-war party leaders, left for Moscow. In London, Beneš fought hard to get his government recognized. He was helped by Jan Masaryk, the pre-war ambassador to the Court of St James, and son of the founder of the Republic. In 1941 Beneš became President, with a recognized government in exile behind him.

In the same year, on 22 June 1941, Hitler invaded the Soviet Union. The First World War alliance, the west and the east of Europe against its centre, emerged again. But this time it was France and not Russia that had gone under first: the weakness lay in the west of the alliance. The consequences changed the political face of central and eastern Europe. Soon after Stalin's Red Army had advanced into the centre of Europe, communist regimes were established in Rumania and Bulgaria, Hungary and Poland. Tito needed no assistance to set up his own communist government in Jugoslavia. The pre-war French system of alliances in eastern Europe, the concept of the *cordon sanitaire*, was reversed. It had pointed against Russia before the war. Stalin made eastern Europe protect the Soviet Union.

A large part of Czechoslovakia was liberated by the Red Army in 1945. Beneš went to Moscow in March, where an agreement was made between the Moscow leadership of the Communist Party and his London government. The Czechs and the Slovaks seemed to have surmounted the difficulty that had made the life of the Poles in exile so insecure. In May 1945 President Beneš arrived in Prague with his united front government.

The Communist Party played a leading role in the new state. Klement Gottwald, deputy Prime Minister on his arrival in Prague, became Prime Minister in February 1946. Three months later, his party scored an election victory, though it did not obtain an absolute majority. It ran the largest and most effective organization that covered all the Czech and Slovak territories. Agreement existed with the other parties on all the major political, economic and social issues. Only marginal problems remained to be settled. The programme of post-war Czechoslovakia was solidly socialist.

In February 1948 the Communist Party made a successful bid for absolute power in the state. Various explanations have been offered as to why it took that step. Because Stalin wanted to close the gap in his east European defences, owing to the increased international tension in the opening stages of the cold war, and the sharpening of the class struggle at home:

such used to be the favourite assertion of the Czech communist theorists. Because the non-communist politicians were inept, and President Beneš sick. Because the communists followed the example of the Soviet one-party state, had no other model at hand, and tried to re-enact the Russian situation in 1917 and after.

Anyway, Gottwald laid the foundations for the establishment of a Stalinist state in Czechoslovakia. In just under twenty years, it evolved its official history and mythology. Apart from its attitude towards the Habsburg monarchy – the nationalists' 'prison of the peoples' was easily convertible into the Marxists' unrelieved feudal hovel – it was diametrically opposed to the view of recent Czech and Slovak history in the years between the two wars. Just as the pre-war writers had tried to excise the Habsburg past, the communists made an attempt to cut out the liberal first Republic from the history of their people.

'Without the November revolution in Russia there would have been no independent Czechoslovak Republic.' The opening shot by the communist historians rang out. The Czechs and the Slovaks owed their state to Lenin and the Bolshevik revolution in Russia, not to Masaryk and the western allies. Masaryk and Beneš had betrayed the people and became 'agents of imperialism', or 'fascist lackeys'. A collection called *Documents on the Anti-social and Anti-national Policy of T. G. Masaryk* was published in Prague in 1953. The first Republic was dismissed as having been run by the bourgeoisie for the bourgeoisie. The communist historians constructed a new variation of captivity, a prison of the workers, which then easily relapsed, after 1938, into fascism. It was alleged that Beneš's foreign policy, that ignored the Soviet Union, led directly to Munich; Stalin and the Red Army alone liberated the Republic in 1945.

Now, at last, Czech and Slovak historians have started to look at the Habsburg past as a rich subject for a detached

inquiry. Masaryk and Beneš are reappearing as three-dim-
ensional characters. Instead of concentrating on Masaryk's
controversial role in the Allied intervention in Russia, the
historians have now turned to his qualities as a democratic
leader. They have pointed out that Beneš, after all, had
initiated the policy of alliance with Soviet Russia. The Czechs
however question Beneš's policy in September 1938, when his
government accepted the Munich agreement. What was the
point, they ask, of such timid carefulness, if the war cost the
Czechs and Slovaks 375,000 dead? There is intense popular
interest in the more dramatic incidents of combat and espionage in the West in the Second World War. The Slovak national
rising in 1944 became the subject of a recent controversy and
started receiving the attention it deserved.

But among the unresolved issues of the recent past, the problem of February 1948 still stands out. It forms a dark pool in
the stream of recent history, mysterious and rather chilly.
The cold war contributed little to its resolution. Caught in the
fashionable, slightly frightened fascination at the communist
successes after the end of the war, students of communism,
as well as the Czech emigré politicians in the West, formed
their own way of looking at February 1948. They saw it as
the outcome of a coldly planned, ruthlessly executed process
of communist 'infiltration', backed by Soviet power and
experience. The fact that, since 1921, the Communist Party
had been a vital factor in the political life of the country, or
that it may have overreached itself in 1948, was rarely considered.

Many Czech communists now feel that the indiscriminate
recruitment of new members after February 1948 diluted and
changed the character of the party, and may have facilitated
the purges. With its newly acquired power, the party assumed
a tremendous responsibility. And as the final irony, measures
against the 'defeated middle class enemy' sent thousands of
people to factories, mines and other places of honest but

unaccustomed employment. The composition of the working class, in whose name the government resolutely ruled, was changed.

Stalinist ways of looking at history had far-reaching practical implications. Statues disappeared from parks; pictures of statesmen in classrooms (they had replaced the traditional crucifixes in 1918) were exchanged; the names of streets and railways stations revised. War veterans who had fought on the western front were badly treated, sometimes persecuted.

The casualties of the Second World War were the price the nation had to pay for its continued existence. But over 70,000 people were involved in the political persecution in the 1950s. It was a punishment inflicted on the Czechs and Slovaks by their own rulers. For the first time in many centuries there was no immediate foreign enemy to blame. That is why their inquiry into the past had a chastened quality about it.

At this point, politics and the past came together and formed an explosive blend. It is the historians' task to find out why their rulers behaved as they did. Nevertheless, the question of the responsibility of the judges, the secret police, and the party, as well as the problem of the rehabilitation of the victims of political persecution, cross the thin dividing line between history and politics. Not all the former prisoners and their inquisitors have made a habit of lunching together.

The strong, tragic memory of Jan Masaryk and of his death provided the necessary link between the past and current politics. Early in April 1968 it was put to the highest legal authority in the country that an inquiry into the death of Jan Masaryk should be opened, so that the new rulers might prove their good faith in regard to rehabilitation. (*Student*, 3 April 1968.) A special commission of inquiry was set up; the Czechoslovak television ran its own parallel inquest; the newspapers took a great interest as well. The verdict is still pending.

In February 1948 Jan Masaryk stayed on as the Minister of Foreign Affairs in Gottwald's new cabinet. Early in the morning of 10 March, the Foreign Ministry boilerman found Masaryk dead, lying under the bathroom window of the Minister's flat. The Czechs mourned in the way they had done in the summer of 1937, when Jan Masaryk's father died.

The death in March 1948 was perhaps more tragic because it followed hard on a period of high hope, because it ended an unfulfilled life. The name Masaryk was now not only a symbol of independence and of continuity. He was at home in all European capitals, and in America. There was not a trace of provincialism about him, he was tolerant and self-confident, and had very good manners. They were all qualities his compatriots could profitably observe. Since the national revival, their traditions were essentially those of the lower middle class, nourished by the sources of hard work and hard-bitten, routine pessimism. Jan Masaryk introduced a touch of colour into their lives and their politics. The people knew that in his person Masaryk combined qualities that were unusual and perhaps incompatible, but that were not their common everyday property.

At the end of the winter in 1948 they found it easy to believe that a man like that was taken away from them. Soon rumours of coffins being carried out of the Foreign Ministry in the dead of night went into circulation. The posy of snowdrops next to Masaryk's head when he lay in state was noticed. His fall from a window and the Czech historical propensity for defenestration was commented on. Over the past twenty years, the event has never quite fallen into oblivion.

The assassination theory was restated, with an air of finality, in a West German mass circulation magazine in 1965. (*Der Spiegel*, 7 April 1965.) The article was used in Prague in support of the demand to open an official inquiry into Masaryk's death. (*Student*, 3 April 1968.) Dr František Borkovec, the deputy chief of State Security, and Dr Jaromir Teplý, a police doctor, came to Masaryk's flat at the Foreign Ministry shortly after the body had been found. The bedroom was, the article further alleged, in a mess: there was broken glass in the bathroom and faeces, the 'physiological signs of lethal terror' were found on the body. Later in the year Borkovec was accused of conspiracy and executed without a trial. The bathroom window was smaller and twice as high as the bedroom window. Why, the author of the article asked, should the suicide have chosen the least accessible window in the flat? Vilibald Hoffmann, another police doctor, found a number of ends of different brands of cigarettes in the ash tray. Dr Oscar Klinger, Masaryk's personal doctor, was not allowed to see the body. He had examined Masaryk on 8 March, two days before his death, and found him in good health. The document containing the findings of the autopsy was forged. Professor Hájek, who signed it, had seen the body, but only from a distance of three yards. Pictures of Masaryk lying in state, with the posy of snowdrops next to his head, were withdrawn on the day of the funeral. The author stated that Major 'Franz Schramm', the State Security liaison officer with the Russian NKVD, had organized Masaryk's murder. Schramm himself was assassinated in the summer of 1948. Václav Sedm, a member of the Foreign Ministry guard, was on duty on the night of 9 March. He left the guardroom during the night, saying that he had toothache. A key witness, Sedm was first generously rewarded for his services and then killed, in June 1948, in a car crash. Borkovec, who went on with his investigation of Masaryk's death, against the orders of the Minister of the Interior, discovered a connexion between Major Schramm and Sedm.

The article in *Der Spiegel* in April 1965 was the most closely argued statement of the murder theory up to date, but it contained some serious errors and inconsistencies. (Its author, writing under the name Michael Rand, was Benno Weigel, who was responsible for another theory disguised as a narrative based on hard facts: the description of the escape route of George Blake, the Soviet spy, from his London prison to Prague.) In fact Dr Borkovec, the head of the Prague crime squad, had a look at the scene of Masaryk's death early in the morning on 10 March 1948. He did so very briefly. He is still alive: his brother was executed in 1948. The investigation of Masaryk's death was taken over by the security men in the Ministry of Interior. No broken glass was found in the bathroom, and its window was at the same height as in the bedroom. Major Schramm's name was not Franz, but Augustin, and he was not a security officer, but worked in the offices of the central committee of the Communist Party. The autopsy was carried out by Professor Hájek in the regular manner. No guard at the Foreign Ministry called Václav Sedm ever existed.

Some new evidence for the murder theory has, however, emerged recently. It came from Pavel Straka, the resident clerk in the Foreign Ministry on the night of 9 March. (*Mladá Fronta*, 7 April 1968.) All the telephone lines but one in the Ministry were switched to his office; the porter, a policeman and the butler were the only other people on duty in the large building, the former Czernin Palace. About 11 p.m., Straka stated, he heard cars arrive in front of the building. There was noise in the entrance hall, and soon all his telephones went dead and the door of his room was locked on the outside. After about quarter of an hour the noise stopped, and then started again about 2 a.m. The telephones were switched on, the door unlocked, the cars driven away. About 4 a.m. Straka went out of his room; the porter, very frightened, asked Straka to go into the courtyard. The body was there, face down, no signs of blood, the windows in the flat two floors above, shut. Straka left the Ministry at 6, and made no report. He telephoned Olga Scheinpflugová, the actress and Karel Čapek's widow, and told her not to believe the suicide story.

In the weeks from April to the end of June 1968 no stronger evidence to support the view that a murder had been committed emerged. Straka himself was dismissed from the Foreign Ministry in 1949 and later sentenced to fifteen years' imprisonment. Released in 1960, he now works in a brewery in Slovakia. Olga Scheinpflugová, who recently confirmed the telephone conversation, remembered Straka as 'somewhat pathetic', a passionate amateur actor. His story has been questioned in Prague.

The evidence on the side of the suicide theory, though equally indirect, has been weightier. Apart from the findings of the autopsy, it rests largely on the evidence of three men: Josef Novotný, the former deputy secretary of the Social Democrat Party (*Práce*, 11 April 1968); Dr Lumír Soukup, Masaryk's private secretary, who now teaches at Glasgow University (*Observer*, 29 April 1968; *The Times*, 30 April 1968; *Scotsman*, 13 May 1968) and Dr Heidrich, a secretary in the Foreign Ministry, who recently died in America (*The Times*, 12 March 1968). They are all agreed that Masaryk had been depressed before his death, and that he had spoken of committing suicide. But there exists disagreement among them as to Masaryk's motives. Mr Josef Novotný stated that Jan Masaryk promised his father always to stand by Beneš. On 9 March 1948 he drove over to see Beneš and ask him for a release from the undertaking. There was an argument between the two men; the President turned down Masaryk's request. Beneš had moved into an anti-communist position, and vacillated whether to resign the President's office or not. Masaryk, according to Mr Novotný, had always got on well with Gottwald and saw it as his duty to stay on in the government.

Dr Soukup has recently criticized the attempt to blame Beneš for Masaryk's death. (Dr Soukup has kindly summed up his view in a private communication to the author.) He confirmed the fact that in his will Masaryk had asked his son to remain loyal to Beneš, and there had been differences of opinion between the two men after the communist take-over of power in February 1948. But both Dr Soukup and his former colleague Dr Heidrich maintain that Masaryk's suicide was the 'final supreme act', his way of expressing disapproval of the power-crazed communist leaders.

Masaryk came back from his interview with Beneš late in the evening on 9 March 1948. The following morning, the family Bible lay open on his bedside table. The death of President Kennedy took place in broad daylight, in front of thousands of eye-witnesses and millions of television viewers. The basic facts of that day in Dallas, quite apart from the broader question of conspiracy, are still a matter of dispute. Jan Masaryk's death at night, in a large, ancient palace with only four other people present, took place twenty years ago. The task before Dr Kotlář's commission of inquiry into Masaryk's death is more difficult than the problem before the Warren Commission. If it proves the suicide theory, the commission in Prague cannot give any lead to the people as to Masaryk's motives and the significance of his death.

The government proved its good faith in the matter of rehabilitation, though the vast majority of former political prisoners are still waiting for it. They are used to disappointments from the past: this is by no means the first attempt at rehabilitation. They had their own club, named after the law under which most of them had been tried and sentenced, K231. Communists and non-communists were both eligible for membership. Political persecution cut across party divisions. The great trials in 1950, 1952 and 1954 were only its symbolic, visible expression.

On 31 May 1950 the trial of a group of thirteen people opened in Prague. All of them non-communists, they were accused of being in touch with politicians who had fled from Czechoslovakia after February 1948. Four of the accused, including a woman, Dr Milada Horáková, a National Socialist member of parliament, were sentenced to death. The biggest of all the political trials followed in November 1952. The 'anti-state conspiratorial centre' led by Rudolf Slánský, all of them communists, were described as 'Trotskyist-Titoist, bourgeois-nationalist traitors and enemies of the Republic and socialism'. Among the leaders of the alleged conspiracy apart from Slánský, the secretary general of the party (at that time Gottwald's office of the party chairman and Slánský's job were not yet amalgamated into that of the 'first secretary'), was Vlado Clementis, who had been stripped of his office as Foreign Minister in March 1950. Eleven of the alleged leaders of the conspiracy were sentenced to death. They were all Jews. And finally, on 21 to 24 April 1954, Gustav Husák, Laco Novomeský and other Slovak communist leaders were tried in Bratislava. They had run into trouble four years ago, when they were accused of 'bourgeois nationalism' at their party congress. The charges at the trial were the same, and they included contacts with Clementis and Slánský. Husák received a life sentence, the other accused various terms of imprisonment.

All the trials, the intricate structure of charges, the confessions by the defendants, were bogus. The executions were judicial murders. They took place at the height of the 'cult of personality'. They followed on exhortations to the party that its main task was 'to increase revolutionary alertness in our own ranks and to unmask and root out the bourgeois-nationalist elements and agents of imperialism, wherever they may hide'. (Ladislav Kopřiva to the central committee meeting, 24 and 25 February 1950.) The words echoed similar phrases in Moscow. Such was Stalin's way of reacting to the final break-up of the war-time alliance, the American monopoly in the atomic bomb, against the belief of some east European socialists, especially Tito, that they could go their own way.

The trials shaped, and were shaped by, the current political situation. They were a way of proving that internal and international tension really existed, and they contributed to increasing the tension. They showed the rank-and-file party members and other simple citizens what the incorrect political attitudes were. They provided an explanation for economic crisis or for the introduction of tough political measures. They resolved the struggle for power at the top of the party.

While the trial of Laszló Rajk was being prepared in 1949, Matthias Rákosi, the Hungarian party leader, gave Gottwald a list of some sixty Czech and Slovak high-ranking communists. Their names had apparently come up in connexion with the investigation of Rajk and the imperialist spy centres in Budapest. Most of the communists on the list had spent the war in exile in England; many of them had fought in the International Brigade in the Spanish civil war. Gottwald at first said of the list that it sounded very unlikely, that the Czechoslovak party had always been legal and therefore not riddled with enemy agents.

About the same time, in the summer 1949, the so-called 'mixed commission', on which high party members sat together with State Security officers, was established under the chairmanship of Ladislav Kopřiva. The first wave of arrests soon followed. The deputy Minister of Foreign Trade, Eugen Loebl, the head of the official travel agency, Gustav Pavlík, and the editor of the party newspaper, Vilém Nový, were among the first victims. In the autumn 1949 a special State Security unit was established to investigate the 'enemy agency' in the Communist Party; the central committee meeting in February 1950 approved the proposal of setting up the Ministry of State Security. Kopřiva became its first head; he was replaced in January 1952 by Karol Bacílek, a member of the party praesidium who did not, however, take much interest in his Ministry. The advice of experts, members of Beria's Moscow Ministry of State Security, was available. They were called by their Czech colleagues, appropriately, the 'teachers'.

Otto Šling, the leading secretary of the Brno district, was arrested in October 1950. His friend, Marie Švermová, the widow of a party leader who had died in the Slovak uprising, was interrogated by a special party commission. She denied any conspiratorial intentions or activity, as well as the accusations that she had played a part in the death of her husband, but admitted certain mistakes in her political work and private life. She was expelled from the party and arrested.

After the arrest of Šling and the investigation of Švermová the security apparatus seemed to hesitate what to do next. Švermová had given very little away; Šling's job had been important, but remote from Prague. In the summer of 1951 things started moving again. State Security was convinced that a good case could be constructed against Rudolf Slánský, the general secretary of the party. Gottwald apparently at first resisted the suggestions made by the Security. At the central committee meeting in September 1951, however, he criticized Slánský's serious mistakes in regard to the 'placing of cadres in top positions' (Slánský was, for instance, a member of the five-man special committee that made top-level appointments in the Czechoslovak diplomatic service). The secretary general lost his party position and became deputy Prime Minister.

Rudolf Slánský remained in his government position a few weeks only. In November 1951 State Security informed Gottwald that Slánský was making preparations for escape to the West, and requested his arrest. Stalin also asked Gottwald for Slánský's detention. He was arrested on 24 November, and tried a year later. His execution took place on 3 December 1952, and his ashes were scattered from a lorry on a road somewhere to the west of Prague.

Political mistakes, administrative carelessness, their private lives, everything was used against the defendants. The charges were twisted into criminal shapes and linked with the 'western imperialists'. It seems that the main task of Beria's experts was to see to the selection of the defendants. They were people with connexions outside their own country, or who had spent a part of their lives – the war in most cases – abroad. Many were Jews. The trials could be linked with similar measures in other east European countries, and the international or 'zionist' nature of the conspiracy established. Stalin took over where Goebbels had left off.

Yet neither Stalin nor Beria bear the full responsibility for the political trials. In spite of their international implications they were, in Sofia, or Budapest, or Prague, largely local affairs, with the party leaderships deeply involved. Gottwald in Prague, as he kept on receiving evidence of 'conspiracy' from his security people, was depressed, and often unable or unwilling to act on it. He was an old, sick man, and now cast in a role that made mockery of his life-long work. The pressure on him from Stalin was strong, but it was more than matched by the pressure from his own comrades. Among the people who urged him to point an accusing finger at Slánský was Antonín Novotný. He became a member of the party praesidium the day Slánský left it. He thought Slánský too cold, too detached, too much of a careerist, and quite unsuited to hold one of the top positions in the party. But it was Ladislav Kopřiva and Alexey Čepička, the Minister of Defence and Gottwald's son-in-law, who played the most contemptible roles in the preparation of the purges. They were later expelled from the party.

The way in which the party was becoming enmeshed with the state bureaucracy, the deliberate confusion of functions and the weakening of the sense of personal responsibility, provided the background to the preparation of the trials. Communists at all party levels became accustomed to denouncing each other, 'personal accounts' for party functionaries were established, and began to gather every scrap of personal information, including gossip and slander. The files were then passed on to State Security. Party leaders and

Security officers together worked out a list of potential suspects, who were then handed over to the Security officers in charge of preparing the case against them.

They used the methods of the twentieth-century inquisition. The Ruzíň prison and the castle Koloděje near Prague were the two main Security centres. They had all the necessary equipment: bright cells which were too small for lying down; interrogation rooms with concealed doors, and the pattern of the carpet reproduced on the walls of the next room and vice versa; house doctors who used drugs to extort, or to fix, confession in the minds of their victims. The loss of the sense of time and of direction, extreme changes in temperature, hunger and its satisfaction were all used to break the prisoners' resistance. The 'conveyor belt' system of interrogation was employed. Extreme forms of psychological pressure were used: threats against the prisoners' families, promises of light sentences as a reward for confession and, in the case of public trials, for sensible conduct in the court room. When pressure of business became too much for the Security, shoddy, bargain-basement equipment and methods started coming in. Iron rods, damp cells in the cellar, motor-cyclist's goggles with cardboard instead of glass, even the weekend cottages outside Prague, came in handy.

One of the Slovak party leaders described his experiences:

I was taken to some castle near Prague. I wore handcuffs and was blindfolded, my usual equipment over the years. Upstairs in the castle there were the Security officers, downstairs in the cellars, in the old potato stores, were the improvised prisoners' cells without heating. It was a cold February. So cold that the guards outside wore fur boots, coats, and fur caps, and they were still freezing. I was wearing summer clothes. It was hot in the interrogators' rooms, the interrogators were in their shirt sleeves, and I was given an overcoat. I sweated all over. From the heat upstairs straight into the cold downstairs. Again and again, day and night. Three officers shared the interrogation day and night, the insults, beatings, threats, the whole planned system of torture. The party sent you here, the party has made a decision about you, confess, confess! Mistake, deficiency, deviation, treason, sabotage! Such is the order of the party. Confess and sign at any price ...

The hand of another high-ranking communist had to be held by his interrogators when he signed his confession.

Confessions by the prisoners and opinions by the experts (on the way the defendant ruined, for instance, the country's economy) were then fed back, by the Security, to the party leadership. All that remained to be done, in the few cases of public trials, was to give the defendants good food, put them under sun lamps, appoint the judge and the prosecution, and fix the date. The first advocate who was asked to conduct the prosecution against Slánský refused to take the case on, and went to work in a factory instead. Dr Josef Urválek, in charge of prosecutions in a provincial town, was delighted to be asked to come to Prague. He was personally assured by Karol Bacílek that it was a great honour for him, that the investigation was being conducted by the best men in the Security with the aid of Soviet experts, and that the party, and Gottwald personally, would supervise the trial. (*Rudé Právo*, 14 April 1968.)

The defendants' confession to the Security and then in the court room was regarded as the cardinal proof of guilt. Perhaps a few of them felt, like Rubashov in Arthur' Koestler's *The Dark Side of the Moon*, that they were rendering the party their last service. Others, it seems, after months of torture, mental and physical, looked forward to completing the obscure farce and then serving a short sentence. The real servants of the party were among the people who had prepared the trials. One of them was later amazed by the ingratitude his younger comrades showed him. 'I was quite convinced that it was in the party's holy interest. They asked me to do it because they knew that I always and in everything obey the party. Even if they told me put your head on the block here, we shall chop it off, it is in the interest of the party, I should obey and put my head on the block . . .' (*Literární Listy*, 28 March 1968.) The idealists and the careerists were united.

When the sentence was announced in November 1952 Zdeněk Nejedlý, the distinguished music critic and biographer of Smetana and Masaryk, the president of the Academy of Sciences, said: 'We should feel, after the revelation of Slánský's treason, admiration for the steadfastness and invincibility of the party. All the evil of which the capitalist world is capable of has been used against it. But it failed: it was beaten and the party was again victorious'. (*K procesu s protistátním spikleneckým centrem*, Prague, 1953.) Old party members who survived the purge made speeches; young ones wrote poems for Stalin and Gottwald. The people were incredulous and excited. The trials produced a mass psychosis, which seems in retrospect, to the Czechs and Slovaks, both incomprehensible and shameful. A wave of antisemitism swept the least antisemitic of the central European peoples; they watched the fall of their rulers, or at least some of them, with satisfaction.

Since 1956, Antonín Novotný and his colleagues have faced the problem of rehabilitation. The way Novotný dealt with it contributed to his fall. The first commission headed by Rudolf Barák produced its report in 1957. But Novotný and the party were not yet ready. The report had been partly dictated, and then criticized, by Novotný. It was described as 'unsatisfactory'. Nevertheless, while Barák was the Minister of Interior, until 1961, a large number of political prisoners were released. In 1962, another special commission was appointed, with the same agenda. It spent several months in a former nunnery in Prague, studying the documents of political persecution. Its findings were disregarded by Novotný. A member of the party praesidium regarded them as a 'provocation'; Hendrych thought they had gone too far. The secretariat then drafted another report, which Novotný read to the central committee on 3 April 1963. Though considerably watered down, it still remained a shattering document.

In 1963 the Supreme Court in Prague quashed the sentence against Slánský, but his membership of the party was not renewed. Novotný maintained that Slánský had committed so many mistakes that he should remain excluded from the party; another executed comrade was not readmitted because he had behaved 'like an adventurer, careerist, dictator and led an immoral life'. Such rehabilitation was degrading for the survivors, and caused confusion in the party; the same streak of meanness existed in the calculations of the compensation for the loss of property or earnings.

The general impression was that rehabilitations were being carried out in an underhand way; a few voices were heard saying that it should include non-communists. The principle of a general and open rehabilitation has now been accepted. It touches on the nervous private lives of many Czechs and Slovaks.

9. Summer Crisis, 1968

Sometime in May 1968 the Prague government agreed to Warsaw Pact manoeuvres being held on Czechoslovak territory in the near future. Throughout July tank transporters, camouflaged vehicles of the signal units, all the conspicuous equipment of an army on the move, was getting tangled up with the midsummer flow of holiday traffic. The extended presence in Czechoslovakia of Russian, Polish, Hungarian, Bulgarian and East German troops was underscored by a propaganda campaign against the Czech experiment.

The Czechs were not intimidated. In the middle of June 1968 a group of scientists asked Ludvík Vaculík to draft a declaration about the past and the future of the movement for reform. Published at the end of June (*Literární Listy*, 27 June 1968) under the title *Two Thousand Words*, it was the most incisive statement so far on democratic socialism. 'The reform movement,' Vaculík wrote,

has brought us nothing very new. It brings ideas and themes of which many are older than the mistakes of our socialism, while others have originated under the visible surface of events and should have been announced a long time ago, but have been suppressed. We should have no illusions that these ideas have prevailed because of their truth. The weakness of the old leadership was decisive for their victory, it must obviously have been tired after twenty years' rule which was opposed by no one. All the defects, built into the foundations and the ideology of that system, must have obviously ripened into their full form. Let us therefore not overestimate the importance of criticism by the writers and the students. The economy is the source of social change. The right word has its importance only in the right situation. And that situation in our country consists, unfortunately, of our general poverty and the complete breakdown of the old system of government; in peace and order and at our expense, politicians of a certain type have been allowed to compromise themselves. Truth therefore does not prevail, truth simply remains, when everything else is spent. There is no reason for a national jubilation, only for a new hope.

We address you at this moment of hope, which is however being threatened all the time. It took several months before some of us understood that they are allowed to speak, and many of us still don't believe it. But we have spoken up and come so far out into the open that we can only complete our intention of humanizing this regime. Otherwise the revenge of the old guard would be cruel. We are turning to those who have been waiting. The near future will be decisive for many years.

The near future is the summer with its vacations and holidays when, according to an old custom, we shall want to drop everything. But we can bet that our dear opponents will not afford themselves their summer repose, that they will mobilize their own people and that they will want to arrange a merry Christmas for themselves now. Let us therefore keep a close watch on events, let us understand them and respond to them. Let us give up the impossible demand that someone higher up should always hand down the only explanation and the only simple conclusion. Everybody will have to draw his own conclusion, on his own responsibility. Agreement can be found only in discussion, for which freedom of expression is necessary, which is really our only democratic achievement this year.

In the coming days we have to take the initiative and make our own decisions.

First of all we shall oppose the views, which have been expressed, that it is possible to carry out some democratic revival without the communists, or possibly against them. It would be neither just nor sensible. The communists have their organizations and it is necessary to support the progressive wing in them. They have experienced functionaries and, after all, the various buttons and levers are still under their control. But their action programme stands before the public, a programme of the first equalization of the greatest inequity, and no one else has another, equally concrete programme.

It is necessary to demand that every district and every village put their own action programme before the public. Suddenly the very common, long expected and correct actions will emerge. The Communist Party of Czechoslovakia is now getting ready for its congress which will elect the new central committee. Let us demand that it should be better than the present one. If the Communist Party now says that it wants to use in the future the confidence of the citizens and not force, let us trust it as far as we can trust the people that it is sending nowadays as delegates to district and regional conferences.

Recently, people have feared that the process of democratization has stopped. The feeling is partly the outcome of tiredness after the exciting events, partly it is correct. The season of surprising revelations, resignations in high places, of unusual verbal daring, is over. But the conflict of forces is only somewhat hidden, the content and the form of laws are being contested, and so is the extent of practical measures. Apart from that new people, Ministers, councils, chairmen and secretaries must be given time for their work. They have the right to that time, either to prove or break themselves....

The practical quality of our future democracy depends on what happens to the factories and in the factories. In spite of all our discussions the managers can hold us to ransom. It is necessary to look for and support good managers. It is true that in comparison with developed countries we are all badly paid and some of us even worse. We can demand more money, which can be printed and thereby devalued. But let us rather ask managers and chairmen to explain to us what they want to produce at what cost, to whom and at what price they want to sell it, what the profit will be, what part of it will be used for the modernization of production, and what part can be distributed. Under the superficially dull newspaper headlines we find the reflection of a very hard fight between democracy and the jobs-for-the-boys brigade. The workers and managers can influence it by the elections to the factory boards and councils, and the best thing to do for the employees is to elect their natural leaders, able and honourable people, without regard to their party allegiance, as their trade union representatives.

If no more can be expected nowadays of the central political organs it is necessary to achieve more in the districts and the towns.

Let us demand the resignation of people who have misused their powers, damaged public property, behaved dishonestly or cruelly. It is necessary to find ways of making them resign. For instance: public criticism, resolution, demonstration, demonstrative working brigade, a collection of contributions to their pensions, strike, boycott of their office doors. We must however reject illegal, rude, rough ways, because they would be used to influence Alexander Dubček. . . .

The possibility of foreign intervention in our situation has recently caused a great disturbance. In the face of preponderance of power we can only remain politely firm and cause no offence. We can let our government know that we shall stand behind it, even bearing arms, as long as it carries out our mandate, and we may assure our allies that we shall fulfil our treaties of alliance, friendship and trade. Nagging and unfounded suspicions only make the position of our government more difficult, without helping us. We can make sure of relations based on equality only by improving the situation at home and take the process of revival so far that one day we shall elect statesmen who will be so brave, honourable and skilful that they can establish and maintain such relations. Anyway, that is the problem of the governments of all the small countries of the world.

In the same way as after the war, a great opportunity returned to us this spring. It is again possible for us to control our own commonwealth, which has the working name of socialism, and give it the shape that would better correspond to our former good reputation and the fairly good opinion we originally had of ourselves. This spring has just ended and it will never return. We shall know everything in the winter.

And so ends our declaration to the workers, peasants, officials, artists, scientists, engineers, to everybody. It was written at the scientists' initiative.

The declaration was published a few days after the beginning of the Warsaw Pact manoeuvres in Czechoslovakia. Though the central committee condemned it and the conservative forces showed signs of renewed activity, popular response to the declaration demonstrated how broadly based was support for Mr Dubček and the reform movement. In the meanwhile, the letter written at the meeting, on 14 and 15 July 1968, of Russian, Polish, Hungarian, Bulgarian and East German leaders in Warsaw reached Prague. It condemned the work and the programme of the reformers and described the current situation in Czechoslovakia as 'absolutely unacceptable for socialist countries' and told them that it was no longer their own affair but the common concern of the states united by the Warsaw Pact. On Thursday 18 July 1968 Alexander Dubček, in a television appearance, asked the Czechs and Slovaks for their support. On the same day Prague replied to its allies. In a firm and polite letter the party praesidium explained the Czechoslovak position without giving way to the pressure.

The pressure on Prague was increased in the second half of the month. The Bulgarian party newspaper stated that the 'threat to socialism in Czechoslovakia is growing every day' and that 'internal reaction and imperialist centres' were compelling events in the direction of 'revisionism and restoration'. (*Rabotnicheskoe Delo*, 30 July 1968.) The Budapest press wrote in the solemn, warning tones of experience. The same thing had happened, after all, to the Hungarians twelve years ago. One of their newspapers (*Nepszava*, 30 July 1968) commented that 'our historic experiences show that hostile forces will inevitably become involved in the process of correcting mistakes and will use every opening to their own advantage'.

After the Warsaw letter, a confrontation between the Czechs and the Russians was unavoidable. It began on Monday 29 July 1968 and went on for four days. In one of the strangest encounters between the rulers of two states, negotiations were tough and took longer than anyone had expected. The local cinema at a small Slovak frontier town, Čierna nad Tisou, was the meeting place. When the first day's talks ended, at 10.30 p.m., the Russians retired across the border for the night's rest. Mr Dubček was unable to sleep and walked the streets of Čierna in the small hours and chatted to a group of railway workers.

The Soviet and the Czechoslovak delegations arrived with carefully prepared statements and with attitudes that were difficult to reconcile. The Russians opened the talks by accusing the Czechs of having betrayed the cause of international socialism, even of having worked for imperialist interests. They had been collecting evidence against the new leaders in Prague since the beginning of the year, and at Čierna they trundled out passages from obscure periodicals to prove that the Czechs had lost control over what was written in their own country. They were not satisfied when the Czech leaders told them that they had never seen the passage and that, anyway, an essential part of their experiment was that editors in the provinces do as they like. The argument about press freedom was crucial for both sides and led to other things. In the Russian view, the inability or unwillingness to control the press showed that the party had started on the long climb down from the commanding heights of Czech and Slovak politics. By giving up its 'leading position' the party, hitherto the guarantee of Czechoslovakia's adherence to the Warsaw Pact and to Comecon, was endangering the Soviet economic and military system in eastern Europe.

The Czechs disagreed with that line of reasoning because they wanted no such large-scale disruption: their aims were more limited, and the promise of a more 'humane face' of socialism strengthened their resolution. The two positions were hard to reconcile. At one point the talks broke down and Mr Brezhnev retired to his railway carriage. Only after urgent, firm and good-humoured pleading by Mr Dubček were the negotiations resumed. On 1 August a meagre communiqué was issued inviting all the allies to a meeting in Bratislava two days later. Back in Prague, Mr Dubček told the reporters that he was bringing with him good news and that everybody could sleep peacefully. At night, some five-thousand people assembled in the Old Town Square. Mr Smrkovský tried to put their minds at rest without saying anything specific. The *Literární Listy* that week published a cartoon of the Czech and Slovak politicians being welcomed at the Prague airport by a woman wearing a Jacobin cap, saying, 'You and your friends, and you never ring up home.'

In the evening of 3 August 1968 heads of the six Warsaw Pact countries assembled at the Mirror Hall in the Bratislava Castle and put their signatures to an ambiguous document that, in one essential point, was a complete reversal of the Warsaw letter. The politicians in Bratislava bound themselves to cooperate on the basis of 'equality, sovereignty, national independence and territorial integrity'. No reference was made to the duty of socialist states to interfere in the internal affairs of their allies.

The crisis seemed resolved. The Czechs felt they had won an important concession. A feeling of high summer euphoria affected the people of Prague; many of them left town for their summer holidays, including Professor Ota Šik, the Deputy Prime Minister, and Dr Hájek, the Foreign Minister. The large contingent of foreign correspondents in Prague and Bratislava slowly dispersed. The few warning voices were not heard: the most thoughtful of them, during the Čierna talks, aroused no response and little interest. In a commentary entitled *The Luxury of Illusions* the Prague *Reportér* of 31 July wrote:

This rupture cannot be minimized. It has left a bad taste in our mouths which will be difficult to get rid of ... the relations with our allies have sharpened to a razor's edge. Even without the existence of the Cominform, the frontiers of excommunication have been crossed. Can we at all hope that it will be possible to return to normalcy, calm down, return to rational, friendly conversation, at least in the immediate future?

It is not easy to come out with a positive answer. We have in fact not committed any of the sins we are being accused of, and we were

not engaged in any deliberate and perfidious liquidation of socialism 'on the sly', nor did we intend to liquidate relations with our
allies and jump the hedge. Nevertheless, we are introducing to the
scene something else, something which cannot become a part of a
propaganda line, but which is the real crux of the matter.

We have introduced the spectre of liquidation of the absolute
power of the bureaucratic caste, a caste introduced to the international scene by Stalinist socialism. Objectively speaking, it is a
stage of history at which every country arrives. But bureaucracy,
even if it has not the dimensions of a class, still shows its character-
istics in anything that concerns the exercise of power. It takes
preventive measures to defend itself and it will do so to the bitter end.

Every system of course has its own establishment, its own
bureaucratic apparatus endowed with more or less numerous
negative, anti-democratic tendencies, which act simultaneously with
its positive and necessary contribution to the life of a modern social
organization. It is impossible to remove it and it is not certain to
what extent a lasting and effective subordination of this non-elected,
technocratic element to the elected power may be achieved. We are
however approaching a point at which this may be possible: we
are heading towards the break-up of the power of this, now almost
hereditary, caste which has been bound by a thousand threads of
mutual corruption and mutual interests with its foreign counter-
parts. Such is the extent of our sin. We do not endanger socialism:
to the contrary. We endanger bureaucracy which has been slowly
but surely burying socialism on a world-wide scale. For this we can
hardly expect bureaucracy's brotherly cooperation and understanding. . . .

The Czech and the Slovak politicians, however, did not see
the situation in that light. Most of them had spent their
political apprenticeship in the party apparatus and they knew
its faults well. They became absorbed in their attempt to
eliminate those faults, and they received the full support of
their own people. They were committed to the cause of
political reform because – and they said this again and again –
without it economic recovery would be impossible. In addition, their party had a different historical experience behind

it from that of the Russian organization. Since its foundation in 1921 the Czechoslovak party had operated in a parliamentary situation, competing for votes, holding public meetings, publishing newspapers. It had never polled less than 10 per cent of all votes before the war, and in the May 1946 elections it received 40·17 per cent of the vote in Bohemia and Moravia, and 30·37 per cent in Slovakia. The party had been used to political competition. The Russian organization, on the other hand, had always faced a difficult situation. Illegal work in the underground, imprisonment, exile had been the lot of the Bolsheviks before 1917; after the revolution they had vast, sometimes unmanageable problems to solve. They always placed discipline and the fulfilment of directives above all other virtues. The Czechoslovak imitation of the Russian manner created, after twenty years, a deep national crisis. The communist leaders then reached back for the lessons of an earlier experience. In doing so, they overlooked the vested interests of other east European communist leaders. They also held an optimistic view of the international situation.

The Czechs and the Slovaks live on the busy, frequently contested, central crossroads of Europe. The passes in their mountains, the names of their railway junctions, the trademarks of their heavy and armaments industries have been familiar to military strategists all over the world. Over the centuries the Czechs have sometimes fought and sometimes worked with the Germans; the Slovaks with the Hungarians. Then, in the last century, some of the leading men in the Czech revival looked towards Russia as a source of strength and inspiration. Before the First World War, two pro-Russian political parties operated in Bohemia and Moravia. For two years after the outbreak of the war parts of eastern Moravia lay within the reach of the Tsarist Russian artillery. At the end of the Second World War Slovakia, Moravia and a large part of Bohemia were liberated by the Red Army. It received an overwhelming welcome and created a new situation. In

1945 the balance of power in central Europe swung over in Russia's favour.

Thomas Masaryk, the founder of the Czechoslovak Republic, had made his mark on the map of Europe when the power of both Russia and Germany went through a temporary eclipse. For a number of reasons, but not for lack of diplomatic effort, Czechoslovakia did not become a part of western Europe between the wars. It was a reliable link in the French *cordon sanitaire*, the advanced positions of the victors of the First World War. In 1944 and 1945 Stalin and the Red Army took over all the countries of the former *cordon*, as well as East Germany, and made them face the other way. In 1947 Jan Masaryk, who had been brought up in the western liberal tradition by his father, said that, 'We have no free choice. Czechoslovakia does not lie between the East and the West. It lies between Russia and Germany. I would have no choice. I'd go with the East. But it would kill me.' (*Plamen*, February. 1968.)

It was a stark choice. It killed Jan Masaryk and many others. But in the summer of 1968 the Czech leaders believed and hoped that it no longer existed in its old, acute form. They believed that the tensions that had started building up in the years 1917–19, and that culminated in the Second World War, were being gradually resolved. The formula of coexistence between Russia and America and the accompanying diplomatic practices have taken much of the edge off the hostility between Russia and America. A sufficient number of signals of good will have been received on both sides and funds of good sense have been tapped in Washington and Moscow. At the same time the old European continent has regained much of its vitality. The Czechs had had enough of living in a state of permanent siege and they started looking for their place in a Europe that was not divided into two hostile parts.

The Russians, on the other hand, share no such optimism.

They know that the German problem has been shelved but not solved. Influential military thinking in Moscow goes on regarding Europe as the most important area of the confrontation between the two systems. An understanding with Washington on nuclear weapons would only add to the importance of the deployment of conventional forces.

Behind Moscow's propaganda phrases about West German 'revanchism' or American 'imperialism' and their various plots, there lies a hard and recognizable reasoning on foreign policy. Twice in this century the Russians have had to face an onslaught from the centre of Europe. Only they know the extent of their losses in the last war, and the country is still run by the men who fought in it. The first Soviet census after the war revealed losses of population higher than the highest western estimates. The vast casualties, some twenty million dead or perhaps more, were incurred in the course of defending Russia's western frontier.

The Russians have no intention of dismantling their defences to the west. They dislike the prospect of having their present arrangements in eastern Europe upset in any way just because, as they see it, a few economists and politicians in Prague have caught a glimpse of the bright lights of western Europe. In their military and economic system Czechoslovakia has a key position. It is a workshop where a lot of Russian and east European raw material is processed; the country's territory forms a tunnel leading from western Europe directly to the Soviet Union.

The Russians are also suspicious of Czechoslovakia's western traditions, and tend to overestimate their political significance. In May one of their newspapers described Thomas Masaryk as a sinister plotter who had been involved in an attempt to assassinate Lenin. It infuriated the Czechs, who had only just rediscovered Masaryk, and they reacted sharply. The historical truth of the matter was quite irrelevant. The Russians saw Masaryk as a man involved in the most troubled episode of their recent history, the intervention by the western powers and civil war. For the Czechs, on the other hand, Masaryk is the unreproachable architect of their independence, of their first democratic state. Last October, that state celebrated the fiftieth anniversary of its foundation. It is a year younger than the Soviet Union. The Czechs and Slovaks thought it old enough to look after its own affairs.

Such was not Moscow's view. Throughout the three summer months, the Russians and their allies pushed the Czechs and the Slovaks hard to keep them in line. They used economic pressure and unleashed the fury of their press. On 11 June 1968 Moscow made known its first diplomatic protest to Prague, asking for a ban on anti-Soviet articles. The Czechs were exposed to a war of nerves. The Russians moved their tanks and troops about at will, reminding the Czechs that, under the terms of the Warsaw treaty, they could do so on Czechoslovak territory as well. The summer manoeuvres went on and on, the last troops leaving the country only on 3 August, the day the Bratislava agreement was signed.

The possibility of a Soviet military intervention against the Dubček regime was raised and dismissed in public several times. The argument centred on a comparison with the situation in Hungary in 1956. Imre Nagy, the Hungarian revolutionary leader who was later executed, was convinced that Hungary must leave the Warsaw Pact. He believed that Moscow would appreciate having a neutral and friendly Hungary for its neighbour. Nagy's second mistake, the Czechs argued, was that he failed to restore order in the country and made Soviet armed intervention inevitable. (cf. for instance *Literárni Listy*, 13 June 1968.) Instead of armed bands roaming the country, the usual summer migration of European peoples was going on in Czechoslovakia in August 1968. The Czech leaders never missed an opportunity of assuring Moscow of their loyalty to the Warsaw Pact.

All the time, two party congresses were being prepared. On

26 August the Slovaks were to meet in Bratislava; the four-teenth extraordinary congress of the Czechoslovak party was to assemble in Prague on 9 September 1968. The way elections of delegates in the regions were going held out a firm promise that past reforms would be endorsed and the way for future progress cleared. But the Czech and Slovak experiment, the attempt to give socialism a more 'humane face', was not completed. The Russians and their allies used the last chance to stop the movement of reform.

Like thieves at night, their troops crossed Czechoslovakia's frontier on 20–21 August. The concerns and fears and self-deceptions of the Moscow rulers were translated into an action of stunning incongruity. Of course no one expects the Russian leaders to act against their country's interests. But they may be charged in the future of having misunderstood what precisely those interests were, and how best to defend them. They used force in defence of ignorance, inhumanity, and poverty, and when no force was necessary. They have in effect asked the Czechs and Slovaks to substitute the old ritual cant for their newly found, urgent and meaningful discourse. They have advised the peoples of Czechoslovakia to start persecuting each other because of a difference of opinion. They have acted against the cause of economic reform that would have, in the long run, benefited the whole of eastern Europe.

A Chronology of Czechoslovak events
June 1967 – August 1968

27–29 June 1967   the fourth congress of the Czechoslovak Writers' Union.

27 August   centenary celebrations of the foundation of the first Slovak high school and of *Matica Slovenská*.

31 October   students and police clashed in Prague.

1 November   Yugoslav press agency referred to the central committee meeting in Prague on 30 and 31 October as 'the most important one in the last decade'. The conflict between the conservatives and the reformers on the committee concerned the state of the economy and the role of the party.

Opposition to President Novotný crystallized around Alexander Dubček, the first secretary of the Slovak Communist Party. The demand for the division of President Novotný's functions was made.

8 December   Mr Leonid Brezhnev, the first secretary of the Soviet party, arrived in Prague.

3–5 January 1968   the central committee meeting unanimously elected Mr Dubček its first secretary. Novotný remained President of the Republic.

29 January   Dubček left for Moscow.

7 February   Dubček and Gomulka, first secretary of the Polish party, met at Ostrava.

10 February   Vladimir Koucký left for Bucharest.

25 February   Major-General Jan Šejna escaped from Czechoslovakia.

13 March	The parliament asked the President of the Supreme Court to complete the rehabilitation of former political prisoners.
14 March	Col-General Vladimír Janko, Deputy Minister of National Defence, shot himself.
22 March	President Novotný resigned.
30 March	General Svoboda elected President.
3 April	a commission of inquiry into Jan Masaryk's death set up.
5 April	the central committee approved the Communist Party 'action programme'.
6 April	Oldřich Černík entrusted with the formation of a new government.
10 April	the central committee of the Slovak Communist Party demanded federalization of the Republic and equality between the Czechs and the Slovaks.
3 May	the Minister of National Defence, General Dzúr, confirmed that during the recent visit to Prague of Marshal Yakubovsky, Supreme Commander of the armed forces of the Warsaw Pact countries, manoeuvres on Czechoslovak territory were discussed.
5–7 May	Luigi Longo, general secretary of the Italian Communist Party, visited Prague.
17–22 May	a delegation of the Soviet armed forces, headed by Marshal Grechko, the Minister of Defence, visited Prague.
29 May	General Kazakov and representatives of the armed forces of other Warsaw Pact countries arrived in Prague to prepare staff exercises to be held in Czechoslovakia in June.
27 June	publication of the Two Thousand Words Manifesto.
14–15 July	the meeting of Russian, Polish, Bulgarian, Hungarian and East German leaders in Warsaw, which drafted the stiff Warsaw letter.
18 July	Dubček asked the Czechs and the Slovaks, in a

television appearance, for their support. The reply to the Warsaw letter dispatched.

29 July   the meeting between the Czech and the Soviet leaders in Čierna nad Tisou opened and went on for four days.

3 August   the Bratislava agreement signed by the leaders of the six Warsaw Pact countries.

9 August   President Tito arrived in Prague.

20–21 August   the invasion of Czechoslovakia by the five Warsaw Pact armies.

Dubček and other Czech and Slovak leaders arrested in the name of the 'revolutionary government of the workers and peasants'.

23 August   President Svoboda's delegation arrived in Moscow.

26 August   Moscow agreement concluded. Dubček was to carry on as the first secretary; the invasion forces were to be gradually withdrawn, but a part of them were to remain on Czechoslovakia's western frontier; censorship was to be re-introduced, and the party was to strengthen its leading position in the state.